Psychoanalytic Approaches to Myth

Theorists of Myth
Robert A. Segal, Series Editor

Kenneth Burke on Myth:
An Introduction
by Lawrence Coupe

Jung and the Jungians on Myth:
An Introduction
by Steven F. Walker

Rene Girard and Myth:
An Introduction
by Richard J. Golsan

The Myth and Ritual School:
J. G. Frazer and the Cambridge Ritualists
by Robert Ackerman

Political Myth:
A Theoretical Introduction
by Christopher G. Flood

Cassirer and Langer on Myth:
An Introduction
by William Schultz

Myth and Religion in Mircea Eliade
by Douglas Allen

Northrop Frye on Myth
by Ford Russell

The Poetics of Myth
by Eleazer M. Meletinsky

Psychoanalytic Approaches to Myth

Freud and the Freudians

Dan Merkur

Routledge
Taylor & Francis Group
NEW YORK AND LONDON

Published in 2005 by
Routledge
711 Third Avenue
New York, NY 10017

Published in Great Britain by
Routledge
2 Park Square,
Milton Park, Abingdon,
Oxfordshire OX14 4RN

First issued in paperback 2014

Routledge is an imprint of the Taylor and Francis Group, an informa business

Catalog record is available from the Library of Congress

ISBN: 978-0-8240-5936-1 (hbk)
ISBN: 978-0-415-65112-7 (pbk)

TABLE OF CONTENTS

SERIES EDITOR'S FOREWORD

In the nineteenth century the model for myth was science. Nineteenth century theorists, of whom E. B. Tylor and J. G. Frazer are the clearest examples, saw myth as the "primitive" counterpart to science, which was assumed to be exclusively modern. Myth, it was assumed, was about the physical world and functioned either to explain events in the world or to control them. In the twentieth century, myth has been regarded as almost anything but a counterpart to science. The subject matter of myth has been taken to be human beings, individually or collectively, and the function of myth has been taken to be other, or at least more, than explanatory.

The psychoanalytic study of myth, beginning with Freud's analysis of the story of Oedipus in *The Interpretation of Dreams* (1900), evinces this twentieth-century shift. In psychoanalysis — here Jungian psychology as well as Freudian — the model for myth is not science but dream. Initially, the aim was to show how close to dream myth is. How myth came to be seen as distinct from dream is one of the ways in which Dan Merkur charts the development of the psychoanalytic study of myth.

Merkur brings unusually varied expertise to his task. He is professionally trained in folklore, religious studies, and psychoanalysis. His wide-ranging expertise is conspicuously demonstrated in the work at hand.

Merkur starts with Freud but then traces the course of the psychoanalytic approach to myth through its many permutations. He considers all of the main figures in the movement who have focused on myth: Abraham, Rank, Róheim, Kardiner, Kluckhohn, Arlow, Devereux, Boyer, and Dundes. He devotes much attention to the neglected Herbert Silberer, who, like other early psychoanalysts, paid the ultimate price for originality: ostracism. Not all of the figures whom Merkur considers were or are psychoanalysts by profession. Some were or are anthropologists or folklorists, and some of the psychoanalysts also had anthropological or folkloristic expertise. It is because of Merkur's breadth that he is able to enlist figures beyond the camp of psychoanalysis proper.

It is also because of Merkur's breadth that he is able to assess the figures the way he does. He ventures outside psychoanalysis to invoke the strictures of folklore. He stresses the necessity of placing myths in their cultural context, thereby attending to distinctively local meanings, origins, and functions as well as to universal ones. Likewise he imports the focus — the fixation! — of theorists from religious studies (such as Mircea Eliade) on the distinctively religious nature of myths. The subject matter of myth is thereby widened from the unconscious to consciousness, and from consciousness of oneself to consciousness of the world around one — though not primarily, as in the nineteenth century, to consciousness of the physical world.

Merkur begins to work out his own theory of myth, one that, following Silberer, makes metaphor central to the enterprise. The centrality of metaphor, or more broadly, of symbolism to deciphering myth has been emphasized by the philosophers Paul Ricoeur and Philip Wheelwright and by the literary critic Kenneth Burke, although none of the three tries to link this conscious or manifest side of myth to its unconscious latent side, as Merk does. For Merkur myth becomes much more than, but not thereby other than, dream-like.

Merkur uses myths from Native North Americans, his ethnographic bailiwick, at once to illustrate and to test the universal claims of psychoanalytic theorists. He continually seeks to show not that the theorists are wrong in what they say about myth but that there is so much more to be said. He observes that especially early psychoanalysts as much used actual myths to confirm psychoanalytic theory as they used the theory to unpack the myths. Like other theorists, Merkur himself tends to use his examples reciprocally, but is always aware of the dual uses.

Merkur chose *Psychoanalytic Approaches to Myth* rather than *Freud and the Freudians on Myth* as the main title of his book to reflect contemporary usage among psychoanalysts, who, for all their indebtedness to the master, view the field as one that has advanced far beyond the purview of its founder. Still, Merkur's book takes its place beside Steven Walker's *Jung and the Jungians on Myth* and makes a wonderfully comprehensive and creative addition to the *Theorists of Myth Series.*

Robert A. Segal
University of Lancaster, United Kingdom

PREFACE

In this volume, I have surveyed and evaluated the methods that Freud and the various psychoanalytic schools have employed in their studies of myths. Consistent with my interdisciplinary perspective in the history of religions and clinical psychoanalysis, I am interested in the nature of myth. My chapters discuss: (1) Freud's use of myths as inspirations for his theories; (2) the classical view of myth as a manifestation of the unconscious, a pathological flight from reality; (3) Géza Róheim's reconciliation of classical psychoanalysis with the cultural relativism of anthropology; (4) the ego psychological view of myth as a culturally shared defense mechanism; (5) Herbert Silberer's understanding of myth as metaphor; and (6) Oskar Pfister's recognition that some myths are insightful and potentially therapeutic. Within psychoanalysis, myth is, or can be, everything from a pathological symptom to a vehicle of healing. In all cases, myths are symbolic, and their symbols have unconscious meanings and resonances.

My criteria for regarding a school within psychotherapy as "psychoanalytic" are nominal, rather than essentialist. My discussion is limited to the several schools that descend from Freud, claim his heritage, and are conventionally recognized within the profession as psychoanalytic. With notable exceptions, however, I have chiefly discussed older contributions. Although I assembled, studied, and considered discussing all manners of recent contributions, I found that they generally did not contribute to the study that I was making. On the other hand, two early and long-forgotten contributions, by Silberer and Pfister, have warranted rehabilitation in perspective of recent work in other areas — metaphor theory and play therapy, respectively.

My topic, the application of the psychoanalytic method of interpretation to myth, is not to be confused with particular interpretations of particular myths. Whether, for example, one speaks with classical psychoanalysts about unconscious sexual zones, or with Kleinians about unconscious imagos of the breast, penis, and mother, or with ego psychologists about unconscious instinct-derivatives, one is working with a single methodology that interprets myths as though they were dreams. What varies among these approaches are not their theories of myth, but their theories of what the unconscious contains. Myths have been interpreted in terms of every theory of the unconscious that is known to psychoanalysis, whether classical, Kleinian, Mahlerian, Fairbairnian, Bionian, Winnicottian, self-psychological, relational, or other. By surveying the variety of existing studies, it would be possible to use myths as a window on developmental theories. However, I have elected a methodological focus to address the *phenomenon* of myth. What has psychoanalysis to say about what myths are, and why myths are myths?

Significantly revised versions of three articles appear as chapters or parts of chapters in this book. They are reprinted with the permission of the original publishers.

The Psychodynamics of the Navajo Coyoteway Ceremonial. *Journal of Mind and Behavior* 2/3:243–257.

1988. Adaptive symbolism and the theory of myth: The symbolic understanding of myths in Inuit religion. In *The Psychoanalytic Study of Society*. Vol. 13, ed. L. Bryce Boyer and Simon A. Grolnick, 63–94. Hillsdale, NJ: Analytic Press.

1993. Mythology into metapsychology: Freud's misappropriation of Romanticism. In *The Psychoanalytic Study of Society*. Vol. 18, ed. L. Bryce Boyer, Ruth M. Boyer, and Stephen M. Sonnenberg, 345–360. Hillsdale, NJ: Analytic Press.

I have also revised a lecture, "Therapeutic Insights in Inuit Shamanism and Mythology," that was originally delivered to the 87th Annual Meeting of the American Psychoanalytic Association, in Toronto, in May 1998.

For their encouragement and help at different stages along the way, I would like to thank Jean L. Briggs, Alan Dundes, Daniel M. A. Freeman, Keith Haartman, Robert A. Segal, and the late L. Bryce Boyer.

1

MYTHOLOGY INTO METAPSYCHOLOGY

Sigmund Freud (1856 to 1939), the founder of psychoanalysis, mentioned myths both in passing and as brief digressions in his writings, but he never devoted an extended methodological or theoretical discussion to the topic. He left only scattered remarks concerning an interpretive method that he occasionally applied to myths. Freud announced the theory behind the technique in a letter to his friend Wilhelm Fliess, dated December 12, 1897:

> Can you imagine what "endopsychic myths" are? The latest product of my mental labor. The dim inner perception of one's own psychic apparatus stimulates thought illusions, which of course are projected onto the outside and, characteristically, into the future and the beyond ... *Meschugge*? Psycho-mythology. (Freud 1985, 286)

In *On Dreams*, Freud (1901a, 633) suggested that dreams were originally "regarded ... as either a favourable or a hostile manifestation by higher powers, daemonic and divine." With the subsequent rise of science, however, "all this ingenious mythology was transformed into psychology." Freud expressed his position more clearly in *The Psychopathology of Everyday Life:*

> *Because* the superstitious person knows nothing of the motivation of his own chance actions, and *because* the fact of this motivation presses for a place in his field of recognition, he is forced to allocate it, by displacement, to the external world.... a large part of the mythological view of the world, which extends a long way into the most modern religions, *is nothing but psychology projected into the external world.* The obscure recognition (the endopsychic perception, as it were) of psychical factors and relations in the unconscious is mirrored — it is difficult to express it in other terms ... — in the construction of a *supernatural reality*, which is destined to be changed back once more by science into the *psychology of the unconscious.* One could venture to explain in this way the myths of paradise and the fall of man, of God, of good and evil, of immortality, and so on, and to transform *metaphysics* into *metapsychology.* (Freud 1901b, 258–59)

Freud suggested that mythology consists of projections onto the environment of what are actually divisions within the psychic apparatus. By reversing the projections, that is, by reinterpreting the tales in a reductive, psychologizing manner, metaphysics might be replaced by metapsychology. For example, the capacity to seek delayed gratification, the developmental acquisition of which is first consolidated around age five and one half years, was the basis, Freud (1911, 223) suggested, for the doctrine of reward in the afterlife. Freud treated afterlife beliefs as fantasies that gratify wishes that reality disappoints. Again, in discussing the origin of sexuality, Freud (1920, 57) turned to the *Symposium* of Plato, which has Aristophanes narrate a myth that human beings were originally eight-limbed, two-headed, double-torsoed, bisexual creatures, but were anciently sundered in two, since which time we each seek our other half. Psychologically understood, the myth expresses the innate bisexuality of the human psyche.

Freud's treatment of the legend of Oedipus is the classic example of transforming mythology into metapsychology. The following passage is from *The Interpretation of Dreams*:

> Oedipus, son of Laius, King of Thebes, and of Jocasta, was exposed as an infant because an oracle had warned Laius that the still unborn child would be his father's murderer. The child was rescued, and grew up as a prince in an alien court, until, in doubts as to his origin, he too questioned the oracle and was

warned to avoid his home since he was destined to murder his father and take his mother in marriage. On the road leading away from what he believed was his home, he met King Laius and slew him in a sudden quarrel. He came next to Thebes and solved the riddle set him by the Sphinx who barred his way. Out of gratitude the Thebans made him their king and gave him Jocasta's hand in marriage. He reigned long in peace and honour, and she who, unknown to him, was his mother bore him two sons and two daughters. Then at last a plague broke out and the Thebans made enquiry once more of the oracle. It is at this point that Sophocles' tragedy opens. The messengers bring back the reply that the plague will cease when the murderer of Laius has been driven from the land.

But he, where is he? Where shall now be read
The fading record of this ancient guilt?

The action of the play consists in nothing other than the process of revealing, with cunning delays and ever-mounting excitement — a process that can be likened to the work of a psychoanalysis — that Oedipus himself is the murderer of Laius, but further that he is the son of the murdered man and of Jocasta. Appalled at the abomination which he has unwittingly perpetrated, Oedipus blinds himself and forsakes his home. The oracle has been fulfilled.

Oedipus Rex is what is known as a tragedy of destiny. Its tragic effect is said to lie in the contrast between the supreme will of the gods and the vain attempts of mankind to escape the evil that threatens them. The lesson which, it is said, the deeply moved spectator should learn from the tragedy is submission to the divine will and realization of his own impotence ...

If *Oedipus Rex* moves a modern audience no less than it did the contemporary Greek one, the explanation can only be that its effect does not lie in the contrast between destiny and human will, but is to be looked for in the particular nature of the material on which that contrast is exemplified. There must be something which makes a voice within us ready to recognize the compelling force of destiny in the *Oedipus*.... His destiny moves us only because it might have been ours—because the oracle laid the same curse upon us before our birth as upon him. It is the fate of all of us, perhaps, to direct our first sexual impulse towards our mother and our first hatred and

> our first murderous wish against our father. Our dreams convince us that that is so. King Oedipus, who slew his father Laius and married his mother Jocasta, merely shows us the fulfilment of our own childhood wishes.... Here is one in whom these primaeval wishes of our childhood have been fulfilled, and we shrink back from him with the whole force of the repression by which those wishes have since that time been held down within us. (Freud 1900, 261–63)

In Greek, *muthos* originally meant "utterance," something that was spoken. By extension, colloquial usage in the classical period had invested the word with the meanings "tale, narrative, story"; but the tales that were called myths generally concerned gods and heroes (Kirk 1974). The idea that a *muthos* differed from any particular version of it lay behind Aristotle's use of the term in *Poetics* to designate the "plot" of a drama. Reflecting the broad usage of the term in classical Greek, Freud and other early psychoanalysts discussed "myth" as a catch-all category that differs from its use in folkloristics, anthropology, the history of religions, and other social sciences. The anthropologist William Bascom articulated what has become the current consensus in the social sciences:

> *Myths are prose narratives which, in the society in which they are told, are considered to be truthful accounts of what happened in the remote past.* They are accepted on faith; they are taught to be believed; and they can be cited as authority in answer to ignorance, doubt, or disbelief. Myths are the embodiment of dogma; they are usually sacred; and they are often associated with theology and ritual. Their main characters are not usually human beings, but they often have human attributes; they are animals, deities, or culture heroes, whose actions are set in an earlier world, when the earth was different from what it is today, or in another world such as the sky or underworld. Myths account for the origin of the world, of mankind, of death, or for characteristics of birds, animals, geographical features, and the phenomena of nature. They may recount the activities of the deities, their love affairs, their family relationships, their friendships and enmities, their victories and defeats. They may purport to "explain" details of ceremonial paraphernalia or ritual, or why tabus must be observed, but such etiological elements are not confined to myths. (Bascom 1965, 4; Bascom's italics)

For the purposes of folklorists, anthropologists, historians of religions, and other social scientists, the story of Oedipus is not a myth. For folklorists, whose genre analyses facilitate the library cataloging of tales, the Oedipus story is a Greek variant of a standard folktale that is classified as Aarne-Thompson tale type 931 (Dundes, personal communication 2004; see Edmunds and Dundes 1984; Edmunds 1985). Anthropologists and historians of religion, for whom the story's function in ancient Greek culture governs its classification, treat the Oedipus tale as a legend. It is not a story about a god, his powers, or the natural phenomena that he brought into being. For the Greeks, the events of the Oedipus legend formed part of the early history of Thebes. Oedipus was regarded as a historical man who had reigned in the ancient city of Thebes. In Athens, where Oedipus was said to have died at Colonus, he was traditionally regarded as one of city's founders, who had bestowed a blessing on Theseus, the legendary king of Athens (Kanzer 1948). A grave near the Acropolis was said to be his place of burial. Other shrines and temples dedicated to Oedipus were located at Eteonos, near Attica, and in other Greek cities, particularly at the locations of events in the legend (Guthrie 1955, 545; Kanzer 1964, 27). Herodotus mentioned a cult of Oedipus among Theban emigrants in Spain. The Greeks conceptualized dead heroes more as angry ghosts than as benevolent ancestors. Sacrifices were offered to bribe them to refrain from harming the living, more than to confer benefits (Harrison 1955). The Greek cult of Oedipus may also be understood as a tourist industry, comparable to the medieval Catholic cult of relics.

Freud, Otto Rank (1909), and other psychoanalysts of the first generation regularly ignored folklorists' distinction between myths, which concern gods, and hero stories, which pertained almost exclusively to human beings. Freud's definition of myth presupposed the once-fashionable theory of cultural evolution, which is no longer regarded as valid. For Freud (1913, 77), myths were products of the first era in human culture, which had been dominated by an animistic picture of the world, but "the details of the relation between myths and animism seem to be unexplained in some essential respects" (Freud 1913, 78). Freud originally endorsed the position of Wilhelm Wundt, who postulated "a succession of two stages of mythology." In the first stage, animistic spirits were venerated. In the second, belief in gods was introduced, causing animistic spirits to degenerate into demons and be regarded with horror (Freud 1913, 25). In his later writings, Freud reversed the sequence: "The first myth was certainly the psychological, the hero myth; the explanatory nature myth must have followed much later.... The life of the heroic myth culminates in the deification of the hero" (Freud 1921, 136–37). In this evolutionary scheme, myths originally celebrated the spirits of the dead. As the dead were deified, myths came to celebrate the spirits or gods of nature.

Although Freud considered epic and saga as instances of myth, he seems otherwise to have followed folklorists' convention to define myths as tales about gods, but legends as tales about ostensibly historical people. In Freud's usage, the tales of Moses and Jesus were not myths but legends. At points, however, Freud seems to have been unsure whether legends were always based on people who once actually lived, or included tales of people who were merely alleged to have been historical. He sometimes described the tales of Oedipus and Narcissus as myths, but sometimes as legends.

For the purposes of classical psychoanalysis, it was rarely important whether a story concerns a mythic god or an ostensibly historical human being. The tale could be analyzed in similar manners in either event. To account for the appeal of the Oedipus legend, Freud interpreted its narrative as the projection of a complex of unconscious structures within the psyche. Humberto Nagera (1969, 73) summarized Freud's theory of the Oedipus complex with the following selection of quotations from Freud's writings:

> *In the boy*, the *origin* of the Oedipus Complex is described by Freud as follows: 'the little boy develops an object-cathexis for his mother, which originally related to the mother's breast and is the prototype of an object choice on the anaclitic model; the boy deals with his father by identifying himself with him.' [Freud 1923a, 31]. The father is taken as his ideal [Freud 1921, 105]. 'For a time these two relationships proceed side by side, until the boy's sexual wishes in regard to his mother become more intense and his father is perceived as an obstacle to them; from this the Oedipus complex originates.' [Freud 1923a, 31–32]

The methodological aspects of Freud's approach to the Oedipus complex may be illustrated through Freud's earliest extant reference to the complex, in a letter to Fliess that is dated October 15, 1897:

> A single idea of general value dawned on me. I have found, in my own case too, being in love with my mother and jealous of my father, and I now consider it a universal event in early

> childhood.... If this is so, we can understand the gripping power of *Oedipus Rex*, in spite of all the objections that reason raises against the presupposition of fate.... the Greek legend seizes upon a compulsion which everyone recognizes because he senses its existence within himself. Everyone in the audience was once a budding Oedipus in fantasy and each recoils in horror from the dream fulfillment here transplanted into reality, with the full quantity of repression which separates his infantile state from his present one. (Freud 1985, 272)

In this letter, Freud announced that he had developed ideas about a possibly universal feature of childhood development. Finding the same constellation of motives in Sophocles' drama, he inferred that the play's power depends on its ability to threaten adults' continuing repression of the desires of childhood. This straightforward line of reasoning from clinical evidence to a parallel phenomenon in a classical Greek drama was inadvertently obscured by the impersonal tone that Freud adopted when writing for publication. In his psychoanalytic writings, Freud routinely concealed the autobiographical features of his discovery. He omitted references to both his patients and his self-analysis. He adopted an ostensibly "objective" perspective that was appropriate to scientific publications in his era. Although he personally regarded *Oedipus Rex* as a *locus classicus* that illustrated the Oedipus complex, he wrote publicly as though his theory of the Oedipus complex were being argued on the basis of Sophocles' text. Far from illustrating the Oedipus complex, *Oedipus Rex* became its proof text.

Freud's aspiration to objectivity shaped much of the subsequent discussion. Logically considered, the validity of the Oedipus complex neither stands nor falls with the validity of any particular interpretation of *Oedipus Rex* — or any other work of art. Yet Freud's adherents and detractors have both repeatedly discussed *Oedipus Rex* as though the Oedipus complex were at stake in their debate. Psychoanalysts have sometimes returned to Sophocles' play to develop themes that Freud neglected. For example, Sándor Ferenczi (1873 to 1933), the founder of the Hungarian Psychoanalytic Society and Freud's personal friend, introduced the interpretation, accepted by Freud, that Oedipus' self-blinding symbolized castration, and that his name, which means "swollen foot," alludes to an erect penis (Ferenczi 1912). More recently, the classicist Philip Vellacott (1971) argued that *Oedipus Rex* has traditionally been misread, that Jocasta knew that Oedipus was her son from the time of his defeat of the Sphinx, and that she actively seeks throughout the play to discourage his discovery of the facts. The psychoanalytically oriented classicist Lowell Edmunds (1985, 3) concluded, "the self-blinding of Oedipus appears a deliberate refusal of consciousness," an act of disavowal, that expresses a wish to deny and repress unwanted knowledge. The psychoanalyst John Steiner (1985, 1990) described the self-blinding of Oedipus as an attempt to join Jocasta in "turning a blind eye."

Freud limited his interpretation to Oedipus' motivation. Other psychoanalysts addressed additional aspects of the play. One trend in the literature reflects the expansion of psychoanalysts' interests, inaugurated by British object relations theorists, to address the mother-infant dyad of earliest childhood, prior to the development of the Oedipus complex. The psychoanalyst A. J. Levin (1948, 287) remarked that Freud "entirely overlooked the effects of being hung by one's ankles — riveted and lacerated — a suckling on a barren mountain side, on a winter's night, and brought up without a mother or father." Levin (1957, 106) added, "On a psychodynamic level there may be a rejection which is tantamount to abandonment even when the child is under the general surveillance of the mother." The motif of the Sphinx was analyzed repeatedly (Reik 1919; Abraham 1922; Róheim 1934; Thass-Thienemann 1957), but most persuasively in retrospect of Melanie Klein's contributions on early object relations. The Sphinx "is the strangler, the possessive mother who dominates her sons and does not permit them an independent existence — the mother who the son fears will devour him and reincorporate him rather than permit him to live his own life" (Lidz 1988, 42–43).

George Devereux (d. 1985), an anthropologist who was also a psychoanalyst, noticed that Freud always interpreted the Oedipus complex in terms of the child's fantasies without giving appropriate weight to the importance of the parents' fantasies and behavior. Children do fantasize marrying the gender-appropriate parent, and they treat the other parent as a rival. However, parents entertain complementary fantasies. Freud's formulation of the Oedipus complex perpetuated the denial of the commonplace but embarrassing parental feelings. "It must be assumed that this continued scotomization of the complementary Oedipus complex [of the parents] is rooted in the adult's deep-seated need to place all responsibility for the Oedipus complex upon the child, and to ignore, whenever possible, certain parental attitudes which actually stimulate the infant's oedipal tendencies" (Devereux 1953b, 133). The psychoanalyst Leo Rangell (1955) similarly emphasized the importance of parents' real behavior. Ian Suttie, a psychiatrist at the Tavistock Clinic in London, drew attention to "the Laius Jealousy…the resentment of the father at the child's advent" (Suttie 1935, 110; see also 134–35). Rudolf Kausen (1972, 1973), an Adlerian psychologist, followed G. H. Graber (1952), in proposing the term "Laius complex" to describe the father's hostility to his son (see also Vernon, 1971–1972, 1972); John Munder Ross (1982) introduced the term "Laius complex" among psychoanalysts. Devereux had emphasized, however, that the parental Oedipus complex is not limited to fantasy. It generates behavior that shapes the Oedipus complexes of the child. Fathers frequently feel neglected and react with jealousy over their wives' devotion to their children. Mothers may exacerbate the marital problem by exploiting their maternal obligations to keep their husbands at a distance.

Several critics of psychoanalysis, most famously the humanistic psychoanalyst Erich Fromm (1959), returned to *Oedipus Rex*, closely analyzed Sophocles' play, and concluded that because Freud overlooked the interpersonal and political power dynamics in the play, his formulation of the Oedipus complex should be abandoned in favor of theories of power relationships (see also Lazarsfeld 1944).

Freud's followers and detractors shared a common method. Arguments about the Oedipus complex were disguised as discussions of *Oedipus Rex* because "psychoanalysis of the characters tends to treat them as real personalities whose histories and motives can be reconstructed" (Kanzer 1964, 36). Few writers shared Freud's perspective that analysis of the play discovers the psychodynamics not of Oedipus, but of Sophocles.

On the other hand, contemporary understandings of literary criticism challenge Freud's confidence that Sophocles can somehow be read objectively. The psychoanalyst Robert Michels (1986, 494) observed, "What we think of as the 'classical' story of Oedipus is Freud's specific reading of Sophocles' unique rendition of an ancient myth." Peter Rudnytsky (1987), a psychoanalytically oriented culture historian, demonstrated that a century of Romantic literary criticism had drawn attention to *Oedipus Rex* and developed the distinctive reading that Freud took for granted. Earlier writers, such as Corneille (1659) and Voltaire (1719), had favored the *Oedipus* of Seneca; but beginning in the 1790s, Lessing, followed by A. W. Schlagel, Schiller, Hölderin, Kleist, and Nietzsche, rejected French neoclassicism and privileged the *Oedipus Rex* of Sophocles (Rudnytsky 1987, 96–97). Rudnytsky noted that Sophocles had departed from his Greek sources in omitting the inherited curse of Laius.

Sophocles' innovation may have encouraged Freud to abandon his theory that hysterics suffered childhood sexual abuse, in favor of his theory that hysterics suffer childhood fantasies about incestuous sexuality. "By shifting attention away from the culpability of Laius — which is, specifically, for a deed of symbolic *paternal seduction* — to Oedipus' quest for his own origins, Sophocles has anticipated Freud's rejection of the seduction theory in favor of the Oedipus complex." To Sophocles, and therefore to Freud, we owe the reconception of "the Oedipus myth from the point of view of the son as a tragedy of self-knowledge" (p. 255).

Freud did not come across the play by happenstance. Neither did he assess its contents, themes, and implied values on the basis of an unschooled reading. Where Seneca had offered a play about magic, abundant in spectacle, Sophocles had constructed a detective story, whose hero tragically discovers himself to be the very criminal that he is pursuing. In French neoclassical versions based on Seneca, early modern writers introduced love stories and reduced the tale of Oedipus to a subplot. The German Romantics instead taught us to value the Faustian heroism of opposing fate, no matter how hopelessly. Freud's claim that the Oedipus complex has universal validity imposes an equally particular, psychoanalytic reading on the play.

Freud's reading was inseparable from his Hobbesian view of civilization as a necessary restraint on otherwise unruly and hostile individuals. According to Rollo May (1961), an existential psychologist, both the Oedipus legend and the Oedipus complex have traditionally been misunderstood by American psychoanalysts, who replaced one of Freud's unearned assumptions with a different assumption that is widely shared in America:

> Freud proposed a view of the infant as destructive ... the "innocence of the child consists of weakness of limb." For Freud, therefore, the Oedipus myth was genuinely tragic. But in this country we have an almost opposite attitude.... The baby is essentially social, is called an "angel" by doting parents and viewed at least potentially, as an angel if only society — and these all-important mothers and fathers who, in the heyday of this attitude, tried to discharge their impossibly heavy task by tiptoeing around on pins and needles when they weren't frantically reading books on childcare — does not frustrate the little angel's needs for nourishment too much. The significant point here is that Freud's emphasis on the gen-

> uine tragedy in the Oedipus myth was wiped out: the external form of the concept was kept, but its central meaning was lost. (May 1961, 45)

The history of psychoanalytic discussions of the Oedipus legend points to a flaw in Freud's presentation. As long as Freud proceeded, as he did in his letter to Fliess, by developing his psychoanalytic ideas on clinical evidence, his use of classical sources was illustrative of his ideas. He was not trying to prove his ideas by appeal to Sophocles. He was using his ideas to help understand Sophocles. Freud approached myths similarly. He recognized that the behavior of the gods in ancient myths provides information about human behavior in antiquity (Freud 1900, 256). Myths are inexact witnesses to reality, however, because they are "attempts to seek a compensation for the lack of satisfaction of human wishes" (Freud 1913, 186).

When, for purposes of scientific publication, Freud instead attempted positive proofs of his ideas about the Oedipus complex, *Oedipus Rex* ceased to be an illustration and instead became a proof-text. In this manner, what was and remains a tenable interpretation was publicly presented as an inconclusive proof. Happily, the more recent shift in the philosophy of science from positivism to the hypothetico-deductive method frees Freud's epoch-making discovery — the Oedipus complex — from changing fashions in reading *Oedipus Rex*.

Working within the scientific paradigm of his day, Freud understood his methodology as a translation of metaphysics into metapsychology. He seems, however, to have made little use of the method. His handling of the Oedipus legend appears to conform with the method; but on closer analysis, the conformity proceeds at the level of literary presentation and not at the level of conceptualization, as confided in the letter to Fliess. Freud's handling of the myth of Narcissus was never more than a metaphor that provided a name for a character type. His third major instance of translating metaphysics into metapsychology was fortuitous: he seems not to have read Empedocles' on Love and Strife until after he had formulated his own dualism of Eros and Thanatos, the life and death instincts (Tourney 1965).

Transforming mythology into psychology leads, at best, to uncertain results. Any effort to psychoanalyze myths directly, without the benefit of historical-cultural associations, dispenses with normative controls on interpretation. Dreamers ordinarily provide analysts with their associations. When interpretive insights provide relief from suffering, their therapeutic value has been confirmed experimentally. Unlike dreamers, however, myths are not available for psychoanalytic interviews. Efforts to rework myths as psychological theories may consequently succeed only to perpetuate myth. A theory's truth remains uncertain at best. The circumstance resembles play therapy with children. Insights that are transmitted through play can have therapeutic value even though the play is fictional and not true. Classical psychoanalysts' interpretations of the Oedipus complex may have been curative, even though the interpretations did not include the qualifications, criticisms, and additions that contemporary psychoanalysts prefer.

2

MYTH AS UNCONSCIOUS MANIFESTATION

Freud regularly credited Karl Abraham (1877 to 1925) with inaugurating the psychoanalytic study of myths. Abraham, whom Freud called the first German psychoanalyst, was a psychiatrist who worked, among other places, for three years at Eugen Bleuler's psychiatric clinic at Zurich, during the period that C. G. Jung was a Freudian. Abraham met Freud in 1907 and they rapidly became close friends. After settling in Berlin in 1907, Abraham founded the Berlin Psychoanalytic Society and Institute in 1910. To Abraham we owe both the basic structure and curriculum of psychoanalytic training and a strong influence on the medicalization of psychoanalysis. In the 1920s, Abraham subdivided Freud's ideas about oral, anal, and Oedipal sexuality into a developmental scheme of six stages: oral-sucking and oral-biting, anal-sadistic and anal-retentive, phallic (Oedipal), and genital (adult). At the same time, he correlated the stages with different forms of psychopathology. Abraham continued to meet regularly with Freud until August 1924. He belonged to the inner circle around Freud, called "The Committee of the Seven Rings." Other members were Sándor Ferenczi, Ernest Jones, Hanns Sachs, Otto Rank, and Max Eitington. Abraham died of pneumonia in 1925; Freud wrote his obituary (Grotjahn 1966).

In his essay "On the History of the Psycho-Analytic Movement" (1914), Freud claimed that "certain typical dreams" had led him to "an explanation of some myths"; but it was Abraham who "followed this hint and initiated the researches into myths" (p. 36). Abraham's procedure consisted of applying Freud's method for interpreting dreams to the texts of myths. Freud had systematically applied his interpretive method to dreams, pathological symptoms, jokes, and parapraxes; but he had addressed myths only sporadically. He praised Abraham for developing the psychoanalytic interpretation of myth into a systematic and methodologically defensible procedure.

Freud's method of dream interpretation proceeds by isolating the incomprehensible portions of dreams, treating them as symbols, and supplying speculative interpretations of their latent meanings. A thorough-going understanding of the dreamer's history, current events, and free associations helps to provide a context for the interpretation. Theoretic assumptions about the likely concerns of the unconscious mind are factored into the interpretation as well. When large numbers of people had dreams with similar motifs, and the dreams' individual interpretations led to similar unconscious meanings, Freud referred to "typical dreams," the meanings of which could be cataloged and predicted, unlike more idiosyncratic dreams.

A year after Abraham's "Dreams and Myths" and echoing Abraham's formulation, Freud (1910b) summarized what previously had been his implicit procedure. Unable to interview myth-bearing cultures as he did his patients, Freud had applied his conclusions regarding typical dreams to the interpretation of myths. To illustrate, Freud interpreted the mythic motif of bisexuality:

> Mythology can teach us that an androgynous structure, a combination of male and female sex characters, was an attribute not only of Mut but also of other deities like Isis and Hathor — though perhaps of these only in so far as they too had a maternal nature and became amalgamated with Mut.... It teaches us further that other Egyptian deities, like Neith of Sais—from whom the Greek Athena was later derived — were originally conceived as androgynous, i.e., as hermaphrodite, and that the same was true of many of the *Greek* gods, especially of those associated with Dionysus, but also of Aphrodite, who was later restricted to the role of a female goddess of love. Mythology may then offer the explanation that the addition of a phallus to the female body is intended to denote the primal creative force of nature, and that all these hermaphrodite divinities are expressions of the idea that only a combination of male and female elements can give a worthy representation of divine perfection. But none of these considerations gives us an expla-

> nation of the puzzling psychological fact that the human imagination does not boggle at endowing a figure which is intended to embody the essence of the mother with the mark of male potency which is the opposite of everything maternal.
>
> Infantile sexual theories provide the explanation. There was once a time when the male genital was found compatible with the picture of the mother. (Freud 1910b, 94–95)

In this presentation, Freud explicitly denied that myths were his primary data. He regularly worked out the typical interpretation of a symbol on the clinical evidence of its use in dreams and afterward applied the same interpretation to the symbol's use in myths (Freud 1900, 351, 357, 401; 1905, 155; 1908, 174; 1909, 8–9; 1916–1917, 158–69; 1933; 1940a). Because Freud postulated that the meanings of the symbols pertained to biologically determined developmental processes, he never doubted the validity of comparisons across time and cultures. Freud (1910a, 36) held, however, that dream symbolism differs from mythic symbolism in one respect. Where dreamers sometimes use typical imagery in eccentric ways, myths are social phenomena and consistently reflect the common meanings of the symbols.

KARL ABRAHAM

With Freud's endorsement, Karl Abraham's "Dreams and Myths: A Study in Folk-Psychology" (1909) served classical psychoanalysts as a manifesto for psychoanalytic research on myths. Like all early psychoanalytic contributions on myth, the essay relied extensively on studies in folkloristics and anthropology that are no longer considered valid. Where Abraham built on psychoanalytic foundations, his arguments retain partial currency, but the result is an essay whose method remains valuable even though its explanatory theory is untenable.

Abraham began by minimizing the difference between dreams and myths. He acknowledged that myths were not the products of "individual phantasy," but he insisted that they were the "phantasy of a nation" (p. 154). As well, he brushed past the distinction between waking and sleeping. "It is not only during sleep that we dream. There are waking or day-dreams" (p. 155). What was crucial, Abraham felt, was the applicability of wish-fulfillment theory:

> Typical dreams ... contain wishes which we do not admit to ourselves in waking-life.... These wishes, common to many

> people or even to all mankind, are also met with in dreams. The first point of comparison with which we must deal therefore is the common content of certain dreams and myths. (p. 159)

Having raised the topic of wish-fulfillment, Abraham took the opportunity to address the content of the wishes whose fulfillments dreams and myths portray. Freud maintained that thoughts undergo unconscious conversion into symbols only if they are repressed. They are repressed only if they are objectionable; and by far the majority of the objectionable thoughts that undergo symbolization prove, on interpretation, to have sexual content. If we grant the validity of these clinical findings, the omnipresence of symbolism in human life implies the omnipresence of unconscious sexuality. As may be expected, it was the last step in Freud's reasoning — the step from the clinic to a general theory of culture — that was most resisted. It was also the most difficult to defend. The logic of Freud's theorizing is impeccable, but it is in the nature of things that evidence of the unconscious is never manifest. Abraham opted for the next best thing: manifest evidence, the disguise of which was minimal. He cited, for example, the legend of Oedipus, who murdered his father and wed his mother. He also cited the myth of Kronos, who castrated his father Uranos and attempted to devour his children, only to be castrated by his youngest son Zeus. The capacity of these tales to arouse tragedy and horror in us, Freud had argued, proves that we each harbor "kindred feelings," the unconscious Oedipus complex (pp. 159–60). On the other hand, these tales are "very poor in symbolic means of expression" because the sexuality and violence are sufficiently disguised by being attributed to Oedipus and Kronos. We feel the tragedy and horror, but we do not consciously acknowledge the desires as our own (p. 161).

Abraham also adduced other proofs of the ubiquity of sexual symbolism. The archaeological record contains an abundance of explicitly sexual motifs. The anthropological record attests to fertility rites that employ a wide range of symbols for sexuality. Again, most languages sexualize the cosmos by attributing gender to nouns and adjectives. In many trades, tools are termed female or male depending on whether they have cavities or have projections that fit within cavities. Ships, towns, and countries are called female (pp. 163–65):

> Human phantasy thus attributes sexuality even to inanimate objects. This indicates the enormous importance of sexuality in human phantasy. It goes to show further that man's rela-

> tionship to inanimate objects is by no means purely objective; this relationship is a distinctly subjective and personal one originating in his sexuality ... man sexualises the whole universe. (pp. 165–66)

After illustrating the presence of sexual symbolism in both dreams and psychosis, Abraham turned to a consideration of the Greek myth of Prometheus, which had been the subject of a monograph by the folklorist Adalbert Kuhn. Abraham had argued that the Prometheus myth had a great many sources, including the Sanskrit term Pramantha, which names the fire-drill. Abraham based his analysis on Kuhn's hypothesis that the Prometheus myth involved "a threefold representation of fire: as fire and as fire-god, as fire-creator or producer or bringer, and finally as man" (p. 176).

Kuhn's monograph also furnished Abraham with a first point of comparison between dreams and myths. Like dreams, myths are brief presentations of ideas that require lengthy exegeses: "The Prometheus myth can ... be told in a few words. The interpretation revealing the true meaning of these few words takes up much more space. Just such proportions are to be found in the dream (p. 177)."

From this fact, Abraham inferred a need for a method of interpretation that "must uncover *all* the images and emotions in the myth" (p. 177; emphasis added). Abraham did not consider Kuhn's methods adequate to the task. Even the best historical-philological research is limited to what was once conscious. What had always been unconscious requires another methodology. Abraham opted for psychoanalysis.

At this point in his exposition, Abraham offered his theory of the nature of myth. Working within the paradigm of cultural evolutionism that was then fashionable in anthropology, Abraham assumed that cultures evolve from primitive to sophisticated forms, the sexual content of which he likened to the development of the individual. Abraham suggested that myths originated in an early era when sexuality had ceased to be uninhibited and was first beginning to be suppressed:

> In the early stages of a people's development, where more natural conditions prevailed and where convention had not yet assumed rigid forms, such [innate, infantile sexual] impulses could be carried into action. At a later stage they were suppressed by means of a process which we can compare with repression in the individual. They did not become completely

> extinct, but were preserved in myth. Owing to this process, for which I should like to suggest the name "mass-repression," the people are no longer able to understand the original meaning of their myths, just as we fail to understand our dreams. (p. 180)

To illustrate his theory, Abraham cited Freud's view of the myth of Paradise: "Paradise is nothing but the collective fantasy of each individual's infancy" (p. 181). The argument is inconclusive, however. The existence of fantasies that are based on infancy does not prove that there was once an era when all fantasies were infantile.

Reverting to the main trend of his exposition, Abraham proposed to demonstrate that the four processes by which dreams are formed, according to Freud, may also be found in myths. The first process was condensation, by which a single symbol expresses two or more unconscious ideas simultaneously:

> The Prometheus myth, which at first sight seemed so simple, expresses a large number of ideas in very few words … these ideas constitute the latent content of the myth.
>
> The figure of Prometheus himself is, as we have learned from the analysis [by Kuhn], condensed from three conceptions. According to the first of these he is the fire-god, according to the second he is the fire, and according to the third he is man. (p. 185)

Abraham demonstrated condensation on the basis of Kuhn's findings and did not here rely on psychoanalytic methods.

Two more processes of the dream-work, displacement and secondary revision, were discussed together. Displacement refers to a shifting or disguise of identity, whose manifest content is a displacement of its latent meaning. For example, the unconscious idea of mother may be represented in a myth as a heroine requiring rescue, and the unconscious idea of a father as a mythical monster who imprisons her. Secondary revision, in the sense discussed by Abraham, describes the changes introduced in the course of a dream's remembrance and reportage. Abraham likened secondary revision to the many transformations and alterations that myths undergo in the course of their transmissions. He also contended that just as secondary revision is simply a waking extension of the work of displacement, it is not important for psychoanalytic purposes whether displacement in a myth was present at its invention or arose through its transmission. Psychoanalytic methods analyze both types of distortion in the same manner (pp. 188–89). As examples of the process, Abraham again cited Kuhn's findings on the Prometheus myth. The Sanskrit variant personified the fire-drill and its production of fire. The Greek version introduced the figure of Zeus, made Prometheus subservient, and so portrayed him in a heroic rebellion representative of humanity (p. 190).

Considerations of representability are the fourth process of the dream-work. Dreams are limited in what and how they are able to portray. The dream ideas are rendered as pictorial imager; it is not possible for dreams to portray negation; and so forth. So too, Abraham contended, the construction of myths as narratives limits the devices that they may use to express their ideas. For example, the relations "as/if" and "either/or" are expressed by similar devices in both dreams and myths (p. 195). "There is, however, one difference: the dream takes the form of a play, whilst the myth takes epic form" (p. 194).

Having demonstrated that all of the processes of the dream-work are present in myths, Abraham returned to the question of wish-fulfillment. Once again, he cited Kuhn's findings, in this case, "that the oldest layer of the myth represented the identification of man with fire and of man's origin with the origin of fire" (p. 197). Abraham concluded that

> the symbolism ... is unmistakably sexual. It gives expression to a complex of sexual grandeur. Man identifies his procreative potency with the ability of the driller to kindle fire in the wooden disc and in the heavens in the form of lightning. The most ancient version of the Prometheus myth is an apotheosis of man's procreative powers. (p. 198)

Abraham concluded his demonstration with the claim that "the myth is a surviving fragment of the psychic life of the infancy of the race whilst the dream is the myth of the individual" (p. 208). Abraham cited several further myths and a great, great many motifs in support of different points of his argument. In addition, his essay contains occasional clinical illustrations. The basic structure of his argument is complete, however, with his account of the Prometheus myth; his argument remains persuasive even if Kuhn's reconstruction requires modification. For methodological purposes, myths are like dreams. They can be analyzed by means of the psychoanalytic method.

OTTO RANK

Otto Rank (1884 to 1939) was born Otto Rosenfeld. However, he rejected his father, who was a violent, impoverished alcoholic, and he adopted the name Rank in 1901. By 1904, he had encountered Freud's writings. He developed a psychoanalytic study in 1905, which was published as *The Artist* (*Der Künstler*) in 1907. Rank became a salaried secretary for the Psychological Wednesday Society in 1906 and continued in that position after its change of name in 1911 to the Vienna Psychoanalytic Society. In 1906, he lectured to the Society on the theme that became his book, *The Incest Theme in Literature and Legend* ([1912] 1992). Rank and Hans Sachs were the only nonmedical members of Freud's circle prior to the First World War. With Freud's encouragement and probably his financial support, Rank, who was highly intelligent, completed studies at Gymnasium and the University of Vienna, where he completed a dissertation in 1911 on "The Lohengrin Legend." It was the first dissertation anywhere to employ a psychoanalytic method. Rank was perhaps Freud's closest continuing associate for a period of fifteen years. Rank was a weekly dinner guest at Freud's home and regularly walked home with Freud after Society meetings. He helped Freud found two psychoanalytic journals, *Imago* and *Internationale Zeitschrift für Psychoanalyse*. Rank entered the army in 1914 and returned from the war a changed man. He married in 1917 and became the first lay (nonmedical) psychoanalyst. He directed the International Psychoanalytic Publishing House in Vienna.

Although Rank was a member of The Committee of the Seven Rings, a series of events led to a rupture with Freud. Jones, who appears to have been jealous of Rank, created a conflict over the publishing house. The departures from conventional technique that Ferenczi and Rank recommended in their jointly authored *Development of Psychoanalysis* (1923) proved controversial. Rank kept secret his writing of *The Trauma of Birth* until its release in December 1923. Abraham and Sachs attacked the book. Freud, who initially liked parts of the book, was diagnosed with cancer of the palate in 1923; he underwent the first operation on his palate in April 1924. Rank quit the psychoanalytic movement, traveled to the United States, Paris, and back to Vienna, before moving to Paris in 1926. His theories of therapy and psychology afterward developed in original ways. He visited the United States annually, before immigrating in 1934. His later work was ignored by the psychoanalytic movement, but influenced Carl Rogers, some American existential psychologists, and some neo-Gestalt therapists. Rank divorced, remarried, and died in 1939 (Eisenstein 1966; Winter 1975; Rudnytsky 1992).

Rank's *Incest Theme* made no use of the psychoanalytic method. The book defended Freud's claims regarding the universality of the Oedipus complex by citing literature and folklore from many cultures and eras that referred explicitly to the theme of incest. Rank claimed that the worldwide interest of both oral and written literature in the motif of incest attests to an international psychological disposition that was consistent with Freud's postulation of the Oedipus complex. Because Rank limited his use of myths to statements concerning their manifest contents, his book did not treat myths as though they were dreams.

Rank first used Abraham's method in "The Myth of the Birth of the Hero" (1909). Published a few months after Abraham's essay, the study addressed tales the plot of which Rank summarized as follows:

> The hero is the child of most distinguished parents, usually the son of a king. His origin is preceded by difficulties, such as continence, or prolonged barrenness, or secret intercourse of the parents due to external prohibition or obstacles. During or before the pregnancy, there is a prophecy, in the form of a dream or oracle, cautioning against his birth, and usually threatening danger to the father (or his representative). As a rule, he is surrendered to the water, in a box. He is then saved by animals, or by lowly people (shepherds), and is suckled by a female animal or by an humble woman. After he has grown up, he finds his distinguished parents, in a highly versatile fashion. He takes his revenge on his father, on the one hand, and is acknowledged, on the other. Finally he achieves rank and honors. (Rank 1909, 65)

Rank understood the hero myth to include a wider range of figures than are considered mythic today. Culture-heroes, such as Native American, African, and Oceanian tricksters, continue to be considered mythic; they created or gave origin to all or part of the world we know. Other instances of heroes can be difficult to categorize. Cadmus' creation of Thebans by sowing a dragon's teeth can be treated as mythic, but the tale might alternatively be read symbolically as a legend about an initiation rite. In either event, what are we to make of Orestes and Oedipus, whose tragedies narrated the origin of further cultural institutions? For Rank and his contemporaries, it sufficed to discuss hero myths as a class. The heroes of epics, sagas, and tragedies were treated together with culture-heroes, and the problem of equivocal cases ceased to apply. As instances of the hero myth, Rank cited tales of

Sargon, Moses, Karna, Oedipus, Paris, Telephus, Perseus, Gilgamesh, Cyrus, Tristan, Romulus, Hercules, Jesus, Siegfried, and Lohengrin. Although four of these heroes were historical men, for Rank's purposes they were all mythic. Rank's ([1922] 2004) expansion of the essay for the second edition in 1922 included additional examples: Dionysus, Trakhan, parallels to Sargon and Moses, Hamlet, King David, Kaikhosrav, Cyrus, Neleus, and Pelias (R. Segal 2004). With the exception of Dionysus, the enlargement of the roster drew on historical or legendary men, rather than mythic gods.

In my view, the treatment of legends as though they were myths, as though myths did not involve metaphysical concerns that are lacking in legends, has retarded progress in the psychoanalytic study of myth. We do not have a psychoanalytic account of myths that explains their religious character, or addresses their conceptions of the gods. We do not have a theory of the factors by which myths differ from legends.

Blurring the distinctions among genres of folklore had additional methodological consequences. Rank treated the tales as works of fiction. He also took for granted that the tales were produced by the unconscious to the exclusion of consciousness. In Rank's view, the myth of the birth of the hero was analogous to the fantasy, commonly experienced in childhood, that Freud termed the family romance. It is typical of children as they grow toward puberty to fantasize that their parents are not their real parents. Rather, children fantasize that they formerly had exalted (for example, noble, rich) parentage and have somehow come to be raised by foster parents. Freud suggested that this typical fantasy is based on an unconscious awareness of the discrepancy between the children's present experience of their parents, and their memories of infancy when parental care was vastly more solicitous. The discrepancy leads to the postulation of two sets of parents, with the original parents being greatly superior (pp. 68–71).

Rank went a step further, adding that the children's fantasied abandonment by their original parents constituted a motive for revenge against them. Rank acknowledged that this was "a bold reversal of the actual conditions" (p. 72). As a rule, children fantasize exalted parents out of longing for better experience of parenting. The manifest content of the hero myth had, however, to be explained. Rank postulated a desire for revenge against parents whose very existence was fantasy, and he interpreted the parents' maltreatment of the infantile hero as a projection. The presence of projection in the tales, Rank wrote, "necessitates the uniform characterization of the myth as a *paranoid* structure" (p. 78; Rank's italics).

Rank realized, of course, that the paranoia motivating the heroes could not actually belong to them. The heroes are characters in stories. The unconscious ideas in the stories necessarily belong to the storytellers:

> This extraordinary childhood of the hero … is constructed by the individual myth-makers — to whom the indefinite idea of the folk-mind must be ultimately traced — from the consciousness of their own infancy. In investing the hero with their own infantile history, they identify themselves with him, as it were, claiming to have been similar heroes in their own personality. The true hero of the romance is, therefore, the ego, which finds itself in the hero, by reverting to the time when the ego was itself a hero, through its first heroic act, i.e., the revolt against the father…. Myths are, therefore, created by adults, by means of retrograde childhood fantasies. (p. 84)

Rank interpreted the paranoia that he detected in myths as evidence concerning the childhood fantasies of myth-makers. He failed to consider another interpretive option. The psychological credibility of the narratives' portraits of paranoid heroes can be explained by reference to unconscious fantasies of paranoid myth-makers, as Rank maintained; but another alternative remains possible. What of the conscious art of myth-makers who drew their models of paranoia from life? The tales do not necessarily address universal processes of child development. They are manifestly concerned with the special circumstances that produce the opponents and killers of kings. Might child abuse so scar an individual as to motivate the politically radical behavior attributed to heroes? More specifically, might a child who has been maltreated by his natural parents, but who receives excellent parenting from foster parents, develop an adult character involving some self-estrangement or confusion of identity, which impels extraordinary action directed against, among others, the natural parents? For Rank, the possibility that folk-tellers are psychologically astute did not arise. He was too busy attempting to diagnose their pathologies.

Unnecessary diagnoses of psychic morbidity were typical of Rank's work on myth. In *The Double*, an essay published in 1914 that Rank expanded to a small book in 1925, Rank was primarily concerned with European literature. However, he compared the motif of the double with ethnological data on the belief in a separable soul, and he cited the

Greek myths of Dionysus and Narcissus as mythological instances of the motif. Rank epitomized the Narcissus myth as follows:

> Ovid relates that at the birth of Narcissus the seer Tiresias was asked if the child could expect a long life. The answer was yes, as long as he does not see himself. Once, however, Narcissus, who was equally unresponsive to youths and maidens, caught sight of himself in the water and became so enamored of the handsome boy so splendidly reflected that the longing for this image caused his death. (Rank 1925, 67–68)

Rank interpreted the Narcissus myth as an instance of the psychological syndrome that Freud had termed narcissism, meaning self-love, an investment of the ego with libido (p. 70). To account for Narcissus' death through an excess of self-love, Rank invoked a "neurotic constellation" termed thanatophobia, or fear of death, "which occasionally leads directly to suicide" (p. 78):

> It is a question of a complicated conflict in which, along with the ego-instincts serving self-preservation, the libidinous tendencies also function, which are merely rationalized in the conscious ideas of fear. Their unconscious participation explains fully the pathological fear arising here, behind which we must expect a portion of repressed libido. This … we believe we have found in that part of narcissism which feels just as intensely threatened by the idea of death as do the pure ego-instincts, and which thereupon reacts with the pathological fear of death and its final consequences. (p. 78)

Rank did not consider the logical implications of his own findings. If the reflection that Narcissus sees in the water is compared with ethnological data on belief in a separable soul, the narrative implicitly concerns a dream or vision in which he beholds his separable soul. In psychoanalytic terms, what Narcissus sees is his self-image, the pictorial image in his dream or vision that represents his self. Whether belief in a separable soul is rightly diagnosed as narcissistic, the myth of Narcissus is a cautionary tale that warns against his behavior. The myth portrays the overvaluation of the self-image that may be seen in a dream or vision. The excessiveness of Narcissus' self-regard is indicated by its tragic outcome in his death. Under the circumstances, it was illogical for Rank to have treated the myth as evidence of the myth-maker's pathology. The myth *warns against* overvaluations of dreams or visionary experiences. If narcotic varieties of the narcissus plant were intended, the myth may have been a warning against drug addiction; alternatively, it may have warned against grandiose or inflated valuations of religious visions. In all events, it was no more an unconscious, morbid *expression of* narcissism than was Rank's study. Rank was not prepared, however, to discover anything other than pathology in myth-makers.

Following C. G. Jung's break with the psychoanalytic movement in 1912, Otto Rank and Hanns Sachs (1881 to 1947) became the editors of the journal *Imago*. Their first issue included a book-length, programmatic statement on "The Significance of Psychoanalysis for the Humanities" (1913). The section on "Myths and Legends" also discussed folktales, with the genres all confused together. Rank and Sachs argued that differences among the genres were less important than the common origin of the tales. "Ultimately, there is nothing else to pursue except psychology, analysis of phantasy life, which manifests itself just as well in other forms" (Rank and Sachs 1913, 37). Their discussion of methodology followed Abraham's position, with only a very few innovations.

Rank and Sachs took seriously the theory, then fashionable in folklore studies, that myths allegorize the sun, or the moon, or the storm, or another natural phenomenon. Rank and Sachs thought it possible that a concern with nature was characteristic of myth (pp. 37–38). They suggested that a conscious concern with nature might play a role in myths that was analogous to the role of "actual material from daily life" in the formation of dreams. Nature did not inspire the unconscious motivation, but provided material that unconscious motives used in fantasy formation (p. 39). They also suggested that the concern of myths' manifest contents with nature functioned as a displacement. The unconscious fantasy materials "are not related to the human family, which would still be too shocking, but are imputed to superhuman beings, it may be, mysterious powerful heavenly bodies, or the gods, conceived as acting behind these, or heroes elevated to such" (p. 71).

Rank and Sachs endorsed Abraham's analogy of dreams and myths, repeating his arguments point for point. They also noted two types of symbolization (unremarked by Abraham) that occur in both dreams and myths: splitting and duplication. Both may be considered subtypes of displacement:

> The mechanism of splitting of the personality into several figures representing its characteristics, also recognized in the dream life, recurs again in the form of the hero myth where the

> rebellious son gratifies his hostile impulses directed against the father, or a tyrant who represents the hated side of the father-image (Vaterimago) while consideration is given to the cultural demands of piety by superlative acknowledgment of a beloved, revered, indeed even defended or avenged father-image. (pp. 43–44)
>
> From the splitting ... should be distinguished the similar mechanism of duplication of whole mythical figures (not merely isolated impulses split off from these).... Just as many dreams seek to fulfill as adequately as possible always the same wish-motive distortion, so the myth also repeats one and the same mental constellation until it is exhausted to a certain extent in all its wish tendencies. (p. 44)

Additions to Abraham's position presupposed the endorsement of the concept of a "collective mind," in Freud's *Totem and Taboo* (1913). Here the analogy of group psychology to the psychology of individuals ceased to be a metaphor and was instead pushed to the point of reification. For example, Rank and Sachs argued that later variants of a myth might be more useful than early variants for the purpose of uncovering the original unconscious meaning:

> Although it is not to be denied that in many cases the more original tradition stands closer to the unconscious meaning, since, with progress of the repression, farther reaching distortions are always joined, still the principle of the gradual return of the original repressed material should not be forgotten; this principle permits us to discover, often in even highly complicated and late formations, as for example in legends, less disguised bits of the unconscious meaning. (Rank and Sachs, 1913, 37)

It is certainly true in the psychology of individuals that repression may lessen with time or, at least, that the repressed regularly return in disguised forms. To postulate a parallel process in group psychology, however, is to presuppose the existence of a collective mind — a single group mind that is shared by generations of individuals.

Rank and Sachs went so far as to locate the collective unconscious. They suggested that a myth "apparently goes through a series of similarly constituted individual minds, among which, each worked, often for a generation, in the same direction in the assertion of the general human motive" (p. 46). Here a series of storytellers, repeating a single tale over the course of centuries, were alleged to have unconscious knowledge of their predecessors' unconscious thoughts, even though none of them ever had conscious knowledge of the shared materials. At the same time, Rank and Sachs (1913, 46) referred to "a stratification in the dimension of depth" that arises "because the myth structure is constantly fluid, never completed, and is adapted by successive generations to their religious, cultural and ethical standards, that is, psychologically expressed, to the current stage of repression." The storytellers who reshaped the myths differed in the degree of their common unconsciousness. Rank and Sachs's theory, it need scarcely be said, is absurd.

A final novelty of Rank and Sachs's presentation is its diagnostic concern. Again, the influence of Freud's *Totem and Taboo* may be suspected. Rank and Sachs (1913) wrote: "Myth and legend formation should be considered ... as a negative of the cultural development, in a certain measure as fixations of the wish impulses which have become inapplicable in reality and unattainable gratifications" (pp. 71–72). Myth, then, is not merely a wish-fulfillment. It is necessarily fixated and pathological.

Writing in 1921 in a survey article on myth, Theodor Reik, himself a lay psychoanalyst and the author of a classical psychoanalytic study of ritual, approvingly cited Rank's views as authoritative. Freud's (1926a) rejection of Rank's *The Trauma of Birth* ([1924] 1929) surprised Rank and triggered personal attacks by Freud's immediate circle, ending a previously close association. Following Rank's withdrawal from the psychoanalytic movement, his thought developed in original ways that influenced the later innovations of Gestalt psychology and existential psychotherapy in America. Rank's writings on myths conformed to his earlier methodology, but now interpreted the birth trauma in motifs in which he had earlier found the Oedipus complex (compare R. Segal 2004):

> The peculiarity of the myth ... is that — in varying degrees, it is true — it not only presents the [cultural] ideology, so to say, in theoretical form, but simultaneously interprets it, so that it appears as a forerunner of the poetic art, to which it is in any case allied by its narrative form. In the myth, however, which a people tells of its heroes or saviours the hero's creative activity appears as an activity of doing (or suffering), while the individual poet of later times finds his true creativity in the making of the story itself. But this profound difference cannot be

> explained only in the psychological passage from the hero to the poet, but springs from a simultaneous and parallel process which transforms the ideologically creative myth into the metaphor, and this survives into modern poetry as a decorative ornament. (Rank 1932, 207–8)

Rank recognized that myths were conscious productions; but because he continued to deny that they might be self-conscious, he never translated his new observations into an appropriate methodological procedure. It remained for Philip Slater (1968) to appreciate, brilliantly, that the Greeks conceived of each of their gods as a distinct personality type; the Greek pantheon portrayed a range of personalities that were encountered in human relations.

THE GAME THEFT MYTH

To illustrate Abraham's and Rank's approach to mythology, consider the Native North American myth that folklorists call "The Release of the Wild Animals." Stith Thompson (1929, 292) summarized the myth as follows: "All game is kept in one place. It is finally released by the culture hero." Each version of the myth includes a host of subsidiary details that expand the basic theme into a rich and intricate narrative; but Abraham and Rank were interested in biologically based features of myths that could be found cross-culturally. In keeping with their methodology, it is appropriate to emphasize the constants of the game theft myth:

> The most common criticism folklorists have of psychoanalysts (and anthropologists too, for that matter) who study folkloristic materials is their failure to take into account the comparative data so assiduously gathered and compiled for the past hundred or so years.... The methodological point is simply that one cannot possibly know *a priori* which elements of a tale, if any, are truly peculiar to a given culture or to a given individual in that culture *without first checking to see if there are cognate versions of that tale in other cultures, and to see what elements of the tale occur in these cognate versions.* (Dundes 1981, 302)

Thompson (1929, 292–93) and Karl W. Luckert (1975, 217–25) demonstrated that the game-release myth is very widely distributed through Native North America. It has been collected among the following groups:

Arctic: Inuit
Mackenzie: Kaska, Beaver, Chipewyan, Hare, Loucheux, Tsetsaut
Plateau: Thompson, Kutenai, Nez Percé, Okanagon, Sanpoil, Sahaptin, Wishram
North Pacific: Tlingit, Tsimshian, Bella Bella, Haida, Newettee, Tillamook, Kwakiutl, Comox, Tahltan
California: Karok, Hupa
Plains: Comanche, Southern Ute, Wichita, Arapaho, Pawnee, Blackfoot, Gros Ventre, Shoshone
Eastern Woodlands: Malecite, Iroquois, Seneca
Southeast: Cherokee, Biloxi, Caddo
Southwest: Navajo, Jicarilla Apache, White Mountain Apache, San Carlos Apache, Chiricahua Apache, Lipan Apache, Zuni
Siberia: Koryak

The story also occurs in a number of variants, each with a smaller area of geographical distribution. Among the Menomini, Micmac, and Seneca in the Woodlands, among the Caddo in the Southeast, and also in Siberia, there are tales in which the hero releases vegetables, tobacco, or nuts that an adversary has hoarded.

Applying the age-and-area criterion of the historical-geographical method of folkloristics, the game theft myth is likely the basic version of the food theft myth, because it is the version that is most widely distributed. Variants in which vegetables, tobacco, and corn occur as alternative motifs, or *allomotifs* (Dundes 1962, 68), have more limited distributions. The variety and geographical separation of the horticultural variants indicate that there may have been several independent retellings of the game theft myth, as plant thefts, in cultures that had mixed hunter and horticultural economies. The mythic scenario, in which a culture-hero journeys to the secret location of animals or plants and secures their release, reflects much the same sort of theology that we find in the ritual drama of a shamanic seance, in which a shaman heals an invalid, whose soul has been stolen by a demon, by fetching the soul back from the nether world. The myth comprehends the acquisition of game and horticultural plants as though they were a shaman's acquisition of animals' and plants' souls.

Alan Dundes's (1987, 168) suggestion that "allomotifs are both functionally and symbolically equivalent" would lend support to the psychoanalytic method of Abraham and Rank. Their pioneering efforts were content to provide a single interpretation to all of the many variants of each internationally distributed myth. In this context, the distinctions among the variants collapse into a series of symbolic equivalences. Whether the theft myth concerns game, vegetables, nuts, or tobacco, we may conclude that the manifest content of all versions of the myth narrates a contest between a hero and a numinous being over the possession of food.

In keeping with Charles Ducey's (1979) interpretation of the shamanic ritual drama, the myth may be interpreted as a symbolic expression of a boy's contest with his father over the possession of his mother, his original source of food. Whether the myth ends happily with the culture-hero's victory, or tragically with his punishment, or both, the myth is a classic manifestation of the unconscious Oedipus complex. The myth's representation of the culture-hero as a thief expresses the guilt that every boy feels for treating his father as a rival. The myth's representation of the father as a mean-spirited hoarder — or worse — expresses the rationalization that keeps the guilt out of consciousness.

To this analysis of the game theft myth, we may append Devereux's (1948) evaluation of Abraham's and Rank's approach to myth:

> Each tale, plot, theme or motif, regardless of how widely distributed it may be, and regardless of its historical origins, has a certain meager, but constant, latent content, which is the same in each tribe to whom this myth is known. This, more or less "universally valid," latent content can be discovered by means of an analysis of the tale or theme in terms of basic human drives and needs.
>
> On the other hand, each tale, or motif, also has a *set* of more elaborate supplementary latent contents, each of which is determined by the culture of one of the tribes to whose intellectual heritage this tale happens to belong. It is, I think, quite evident that just as the "identical" dreams of two persons cannot have identical latent contents, so a Trickster story cannot have the same latent meaning for a boisterous Mohave addicted to practical jokes, as for a relatively restrained Zuni Indian. (p. 235)

Devereux reflected the consensus among anthropologists when he suggested that the universal features of myths do not begin to exhaust the tales' points of interest.

3

MYTH AND THE BASIC DREAM

The psychoanalytic study of myth underwent dramatic change when it was taken up by Géza Róheim (1891 to 1953), the first anthropologist who trained as a psychoanalyst. Myths ceased to be treated as exclusively literary texts and began to be studied in living cultural use.

Having developed an avid interest in folklore and anthropology during his teenage years, Róheim studied with Karl Weule at the University of Leipzig and Felix von Luschau at the University of Berlin. In 1912, he took his degree in geography, with a minor in anthropology, because degrees in anthropology were then unavailable on the European continent. In 1915, he began psychoanalytic training with Ferenczi at the Budapest Institute of Psychoanalysis and invented the term psychoanalytic anthropology. In 1919, when a chair of anthropology was established at the University of Budapest, Róheim became its first holder. In 1921, Freud gave Róheim's article, "Australian Totemism," the prize for the year's best article on applied psychoanalysis. With finances supplied by Princess Marie Bonaparte, Róheim conducted his first fieldwork in 1929 to 1931, in Central Australia, on Normanby Island in Melanesia, in Somaliland in East Africa, and among the Yuma Indians of Arizona. Róheim emigrated to the United States in 1938. He worked as a clinician, initially at Worcester State Hospital and from the early 1940s onward in private practice in New York. In 1947, with the assistance of the anthropologist Clyde Kluckhohn, Róheim conducted fieldwork among the Navajo. He died in 1953, shortly after the death of his wife Ilona (Devereux 1953a; La Barre 1966; Robinson 1969; Muensterberger and Nichols 1974).

THE CULTURAL CONTEXT OF SYMBOLISM

Róheim was a classical psychoanalyst who took for granted the psychic unity of humankind (Róheim 1950, 435). Róheim acknowledged only a limited form of cultural relativity. Freud (1925, 68–69) complimented both his orthodoxy and his originality in remarking that Róheim, together with Reik, "took up the line of thought which I developed in *Totem and Taboo* and extended it, deepened it, or corrected it." Cultural relativity first impacted on psychoanalysis when Bronislaw Malinowski (1924, 1927), a pioneer of anthropological fieldwork and an early supporter of psychoanalysis among professional anthropologists, cited the role of mothers' brothers in the Trobriand Islands as evidence of the universality of the Oedipus complex. Malinowski had thought that he was supporting Freud when he maintained that the matrilineal social structure displaced the boys' hostility for the father onto the maternal uncle. However, the psychoanalyst Ernest Jones, acting for Freud, found Malinowski's conclusion unacceptable. Jones insisted that the Oedipus complex pertained to the biological father (Parsons 1969; Spiro 1982, 1984; Wax 1990). Because the Oedipus complex develops out of the "primal scene" fantasy, which concerns the child's conception by its parents (Green 1986, 158), Freud's theory necessarily concerns the biological parents. The Oedipus complex is not claimed to be a socially based fantasy concerning the child's actual living arrangements. Were it so, there would be no reason for it to be unconscious. Because Malinowski had intended to support Freud while adjusting psychoanalytic theory to accommodate anthropologists' convictions regarding cultural relativism, Jones's defense of Freud's theory appeared to anthropologists as dogmatic, unimaginative, and unacceptably amateurish. The feeling was mutual, however. Malinowski's failure to grasp the interior logic of Freudian theory left psychoanalysts unimpressed with anthropological claims about cultural relativism.

In Róheim's view, cultural relativism, in the sense advocated by Malinowski, was provably wrong. He cited Trobriand Island myths, collected by Malinowski, in which sons kill their fathers and have intercourse with their mothers (Ingram 1963; Spiro 1982; Dundes 1992). Malinowski's interpretation of Trobriand Island data was independently challenged by other anthropologists (Lancaster 1932), and the evidence for Oedipal motifs in world folklore and culture is overwhelming

(Stephens 1962; Spiro 1973, 1982, 1984; Ramanujan 1984; Johnson and Price-Williams 1996). The psychoanalytic anthropologist Melford E. Spiro (1982) concluded a closely argued, book-length demolition of Malinowski's construction of his field data with the observation: "If this report ["of the putative Trobriand Island matrilineal complex"] had been subjected to the probing scrutiny to which anomalous findings are usually subject, the matrilineal complex would have been rejected ... as empirically unsupported rather than achieving the status of an incontrovertible finding of anthropological science" (p. 179). Róheim's refutation of Malinowski, by appeal to Malinowski's publications on Trobriand Island myths, should have ended the debate. Instead, Malinowski's position continues to be promoted dogmatically in anthropology; for example, by Gananath Obeyesekere (1990), who confuses manifest and latent in his handling of Hindu myths when he argues that an extended series of displacements so alters the Oedipus complex that it ceases to be Oedipal. (On Oedipal tales in India, see Ramanujan 1984; Vaidyanathan and Kripal 1999).

Róheim objected on equally empirical grounds to Malinowski's denial of anal eroticism in the Trobriands. Róheim wrote:

> [Malinowski] told anthropologists that among the Trobriand Islanders there was no anal eroticism.
>
> When I visited Freud before I left for my fieldwork I repeated this passage. His reply was so characteristic that I quote it verbatim: "*Was, haben denn die Leute keinen Anus*?" ["What! Don't these people have an anus?"] Well, they have one. When in the field I discussed the matter with some of the white traders who had had plenty of experience with women in the Trobriands and on Normanby. They told me, of course, such a reply is what the natives would give Malinowski, and they said I would get the decisive data from one of the judges in the Trobriands. I wrote to Judge Bellamy, and he confirmed what the trader had already said. Many native women had been coming to the Judge to ask whether according to the white man's law they would be obliged to let their husbands have intercourse with them *per rectum*. (Róheim 1950, 159)

Róheim's commitment to Freud's (1905) extension of the concept of sexuality, as additionally developed by Abraham and Ferenczi, was fundamental to his psychoanalytic work. Symbols were always to be understood in a psychoanalytic sense as sexually motivated flights from reality. "Our fantasy helps us to endure reality by denying it" (Róheim 1945, 8). Róheim also made selected use of the object relations theories developed by Melanie Klein, but he remained largely unaffected by ego psychology as developed by Anna Freud, Heinz Hartmann, and others.

Although Róheim opposed cultural relativism, he rejected theories of the inborn nature of symbolism. Psychoanalytic anthropology, as he conceived it, agreed with the anthropological consensus that symbols are local and conventional. As a psychoanalyst Róheim insisted, however, that the unconscious meanings of symbols are universal:

> Do we believe like Jung and also Freud that symbols are inherited? Does every human being inherit symbolism of the penis as a snake or the vagina as a cave? I certainly do not hold this belief. But I do believe that the disposition to form symbols is inherited and the symbolism itself is based on the child-mother situation. In this situation the child's environment is mother and the environmental is libidinal. Hence we develop the tendency to *cathect* environment in general with libido. That all erect or penetrating objects should be used as male symbols and all receiving objects as female symbols is evident....we cannot prove that equations like snake-phallos are correlated with any particular type of culture or of society or of personality. (Róheim 1950, 444)

Róheim's approach to symbolism had methodological consequences. When dealing with cultural symbols, one could not generalize about universal meanings. Neither could one interpret cultural symbols by extrapolating, as other analysts tended to do, from symbols' meanings in the dreams of analysands in other cultures. The only way to get at the meaning of a culture's symbols was to immerse oneself in the specific culture's symbols:

> What I mean by a "potentially universal" symbol is that since anyone *may* form such a symbol connection, it would be impossible to prove any connection between it and a specific character type or social organization. The interpretation must be based on the "associations," that is, upon the cluster of customs or myths or their variants, if it is not openly given by the narrator. But this is not a culture-bound interpretation, and one can have nightmares whatever language one speaks! (Róheim 1950, 23)

> It is evident that views on the religion of primitive tribes have absolutely no value unless supported by mythological data and that our hope of a valid explanation increases in a direct ratio with the number of myths and variants. (Róheim 1972, 8)

In addition to these statements about extensive familiarization with each culture's use of symbols, Róheim occasionally referred to interpreting cultures' symbols by asking informants from those cultures to free associate to occurrences of the symbols in their dreams.

THE ONTOGENETIC THEORY OF CULTURE

Like many anthropologists, Róheim was primarily concerned with the phenomenon of culture. Myth was a lifelong subsidiary interest that he initially discussed as a component of culture but later came to address as a distinctive phenomenon on its own. In keeping with Sir E. B. Tylor, Sir J. G. Frazer, and other leading anthropologists of the late nineteenth century, Freud and his first psychoanalytic coworkers never doubted the theory of cultural evolution. However, Freud had added the postulates of a collective mind and a prehistoric fantasy about the rebellion of sons against their tyrannical father. Freud expressed the latter in the final chapter of *Totem and Taboo*, where he offered a theory of the origin of totemism. It is a speculation regarding prehistory:

> In Darwin's [theory of the] primal horde.... there is a violent and jealous father who keeps all the females for himself and drives away his sons as they grow up.... One day the brothers who had been driven out came together, killed and devoured their father and so made an end of the patriarchal horde. United, they had the courage to do and succeeded in doing what would have been impossible for them individually.... Cannibal savages as they were, it goes without saying that they devoured their victim as well as killing him. The violent primal father had doubtless been the feared and envied model of each one of the company of brothers; and in the act of devouring him they accomplished their identification with him, and each one of them acquired a portion of his strength....
>
> After they had got rid of him, had satisfied their hatred and had put into effect their wish to identify themselves with him, the affection which had all this time been pushed under was

> bound to make itself felt. It did so in the form of remorse. A sense of guilt made its appearance, which in this instance coincided with the remorse felt by the whole group.... They revoked their deed by forbidding the killing of the totem, the substitute for their father; and they renounced its fruits by resigning their claim to the women who had now been set free. (Freud 1913, 141–43)

These events were the basis, Freud (1913, 156) argued, for "the beginnings of religion, morality, society and art." Freud (1921, 134, 140) later termed it "the scientific myth of the father of the primal horde ... our myth of the primal family." Although Freud made the theory account for both hypnosis (1921, 122–25, 127, 135–37, 139–41) and the origin of the superego (1923a, 38), it had no bearing on the clinical practice of psychoanalysis and generally went unremarked by clinicians.

Anthropologists treated it less kindly. Beginning in the 1890s with Franz Boas and Alfred L. Kroeber, the American school of cultural anthropology devoted itself to fieldwork. Through Bronislaw Malinowski and Alfred R. Radcliffe-Brown, British social anthropology followed suit in the years following World War I. The validity of totemism as a cross-cultural phenomenon was demolished by Alexander A. Goldenweiser in 1910. Freud's armchair speculations about totemism and cultural evolution were passé even as his book went to press; and the idiosyncrasies of his theory made it still less acceptable (for a thorough account of Freud's use of anthropology, see Wallace 1983). As the anthropologist and psychoanalyst Robert Paul (1976, 312) remarked, "no one (except the early Róheim) has ever accepted a literal reading of Freud's tale of the primal crime, and at the same time professed to be a member of the anthropological community."

Róheim initially assumed the validity of Freud's theory. His first major work, *Australian Totemism* (1925), was a systematic effort to sustain Freud's theories about totemism, ritual, myth, and magic, in a close review of the literature on aboriginal Australian religion. In the course of the book, Róheim demonstrated, however, that psychoanalytic anthropologists could proceed much as clinicians did by ignoring Freud's theories about prehistory without directly challenging them.

Methodologically, Róheim aligned himself with Abraham. In aboriginal Australian cultures, the primordial era of the ancestors is termed the dreaming or dreamtime (Stanner 1956); and Róheim (1925, 46) cited the Australian concept as license for Abraham's methodology: "As its principal hero is actually made responsible for a dream experience we may try and explain the legend according to the principles of dream-interpretation." Interpreting myths as though they were dreams, Róheim found that he could interpret myths in terms of both the primal crime of Freud's prehistoric speculation and the Oedipus complex of contemporary clinical observation. Phylogeny, the origin of the species, was at one with ontogeny, the development of the individual. "Myths are records of the past, both of onto- and phylogenesis" (p. 312).

Róheim rejected Freud's postulates of a collective mind and the inheritance of unconscious memories. He instead maintained that knowledge of prehistoric events was transmitted by living cultural traditions in the form of folklore:

> There seems good reason to suppose that humanity inherited from its semi-brutal ancestors the form of society which has been called the Cyclopean family; a number of young males, young and adult females roaming about on a restricted area under the leadership of a single full-grown male. In this state of society, tribe, clan and family are co-extensive units; or rather, the Cyclopean family (or horde) is the germ out of which these institutions are differentiated in the course of evolution. Legend seems to have conserved the traces of this stage of social origins....
>
> The next stage in the evolution of humanity is the conflict between Old and Young, between the jealous Father and the grown-up Son, the prize of the victor — the cause of the conflict — being the women of the horde, the mothers, sisters, and daughters. Now there is a class of myths.... the details of which seem to be explicable by this great primeval battle of social evolution. (Róheim 1925, 37–38)

Interestingly, when Róheim (1925, 104–5, 107–8, 110–11) interpreted Australian myths in terms of Freud's theories of the primal horde, the primal crime, and so forth, he implied that tales which claimed to narrate events of the distant past were to be treated at face value as legends that remembered aspects of actual prehistoric events:

> [The Australians] represent a phase of totemism prior to the contrition which followed the great prehistoric parricide: indeed, this can not well be otherwise, as they themselves are the "Fathers" and their positive totemism is primarily but a

> psychical reflection of the physical feeling of unity with the environment.
>
> Yet we cannot doubt that innumerable strata of human development are superposed on each other in these myths: the "Fathers" of the present race are also the "Primeval Sons" who have killed and devoured the "Primeval Sire" and who now continue to repeat the deed in sacramentally eating the totem. (Róheim, 1925, 101)

This formulation obliterated the distinction between myths and legends. The Australian narratives were not to be understood in the conventional manner as fictional tales about the primordial activities of divine beings. They were remembrances of the prehistoric past, as legends are. A similar complexity attended rituals.

> On the one hand tradition is an exaggerated projection of the tendencies embodied in ritual into the phylogenetic past; but on the other hand ritual itself is a reduced repetition of the tendencies that actually dominated the phylo- and ontogenetic past so that the traditions are history after all, but reflected through the double mirror of backward projection. (Róheim 1925, 117)

Róheim began to correct himself a third of the way into the book, where he drew a methodological conclusion that inadvertently put paid to Freud's theories of prehistory. It was logically impossible that myths could remember a time prior to the mutation of the species. "There can be no question of a direct survival of phylogenesis in myth" (p. 133). The apparent memory might be attributed to "a brief recapitulation" of phylogeny in ontogenesis (p. 133), but it might instead be attributed to a projection of the present into the distant past. "The general tendency is the projection of ontogenetic into phylogenetic beginnings" (p. 138). In either event, it was necessary and sufficient to interpret Australian myths in terms of the development of contemporary individuals. "All the culture heroes who teach the natives the elements of their present social organization are evidently reflections of the part played by the father in the individual life; it is from him that the child learns the common arts of life as well as how to behave in accordance with tribal law" (p. 134).

The Australian tales were now myths and no longer to be mistaken as legends.

Róheim saw the relation of myth and ritual as a necessary one. Both reflect unconscious psychic life:

> There is no such thing as "inventing" myths; psychic life is governed by the same strict laws that obtain elsewhere. In the myths that originate in the reaction of the Unconscious to existing institutions we see but a reflection of those unconscious mechanisms that led to the origin of these same institutions. The various myths that account for the origin of totemism are all true, but they represent various stages of psychic regression, that is more pristine and more recent forms of the mental attitudes which are condensed in the institution of totemism. (pp. 137–38)

Róheim first reported his fieldwork of 1929 to 1931 in a book-length article, "Psycho-Analysis of Primitive Cultural Types" (1932), which was published in *International Journal of Psycho-Analysis*. Midway through the text, Róheim advanced an original theory on which psychoanalytic anthropology has depended ever since. Róheim suggested that differences in the practices of child-rearing are reflected by corresponding differences in cultures as wholes.

> Every society has a characteristic feature, something which strikes the eye of a human being who comes from another society. It seems probable that these peculiarities — from the outsider's point of view — have their roots in tendencies which are universally human, yet particularly accentuated in the group in question. (Róheim 1932, 121)

> Civilization in general is evolved from the process of defence against the primal instinctual demands and takes the shape of a specific culture as a mode of defence against a typical infantile trauma.... it may be regarded as a more or less specific trauma according to the varying behaviour of the parents. We may equally view as traumata either an excessively pleasurable situation, or a deprivation or frustration, or a too aggressive attitude on the parents' part.... every culture takes its specific colour from a compromise arrived at between the super-ego, as a more or less constant unity, on the one side, and the governing trauma on the other. This compromise is embodied in a group-ideal. (pp. 196–97)

To illustrate the theory he was advancing, Róheim cited the *alknarintja* myths of Central Australian aborigines. "These are women who will not look at men, who are 'wild' and run away at the sight of a male being. It is the greatest ambition and achievement of an Aranda if he can either by magic or by sheer force subdue one of these women into obedience" (p. 49). Analyzing an old Aranda man's dream of a group of *alknarintja* women (pp. 49–50), Róheim concluded that "the woman who refuses all men is the mother, both because she is inaccessible to the desires of her son and because he would like her to be inaccessible to the love-making of his father" (p. 51). Róheim also noted a belief associated with the mythological character.

> If you dream of an *alknarintja* woman approaching, you must speedily awake. Why? Because she will make a man lie on his back and she will then sit on his penis. The *alknarintja* then cohabits with the man, but she takes the role of the male and makes the man play the part of the female. (p. 53)

Róheim remarked that the fantasy of the mother with the penis is widespread cross-culturally. The detail of the *alknarintja*'s activities made sense, however, when Róheim learned that mothers routinely lay on top of small children while they slept to protect the children from the attacks of predatory animals. "They even added, to make things clearer, that she lies on the child like the male on the female in cohabitation" (p. 54).

Róheim reasoned that small boys would routinely be overstimulated and traumatized by the close proximity of their mothers during their Oedipal phases. "The danger for the immature ego consists in a too great approximation to the primary wishes" (p. 93). "A full gratification" of the boys' incestuous wishes "would not be tolerated by either parent and would also be made impossible ... by the superego" (p. 94). As a result, the idea of an Oedipal victory, a boy's incestuous relation with his mother, would be repressed, and the fixation would result in the formation of symptoms such as the child-eating *alknarintja* woman (p. 93), that fused the realistic danger of being eaten by a predator with the psychological danger of mother's sexual proximity. Calling the *alknarintja* "the *specific symptom* of Central Australian psychology" (p. 117), Róheim suggested, among other things, that the developmental trauma of incestuous overstimulation also underlay other cultural symbols. He interpreted the initiation rite of subincision, which involves the longitudinal splitting of the penis, as the creation of a vagina within the penis; and he suggested that men's appropriation of the vagina in "a symbolical coitus in the absence of the female" (p. 118) was responsive to the fear of sexual predation by women.

Róheim consolidated and extended his previous contributions in *The Riddle of the Sphinx* (1934). It was methodologically necessary to acknowledge the adequacy of ontogenetic interpretations of cultures in terms of individual developments. There was no need to indulge speculations regarding prehistory:

> If we attempt to derive the specific traits of individual cultures from the infantile experience of the individuals who live in these cultures, we must admit the possibility of describing the origin of culture in general in ontogenetic terms, that is, of deriving it from a specifically human form of childhood, from a permanent, universal, and at the same time historic, cause. (Róheim 1934, 159)

Moreover, there was an element of illogic in Freud's theory of the primal crime. If the brothers had no superegos, how was it that they felt remorse over parricide? "We may also suppose that the ontogenetic factor was already operative" (Róheim 1934, 177). "One must assume that the sons' ambivalent relation to their father was already present at this epoch" (p. 186). Freud's time scheme was wrong. The evolution of superegos had to be dated much earlier than the origin of totemism, ritual, myth, and so forth. "The apes described by Zuckerman had already gone a long way upon the road" (p. 189). In these reflections, Róheim anticipated recent efforts to revive Freud's theory of the primal horde by dating the events to primate rather than hominid evolution (Badcock 1980). Such a reformulation detaches the theory of the primal horde from theories of the origin of religion, which paleoanthropologists currently date to the Neanderthal period, comparatively late in the evolution of hominids. "The view that the myths are really memories of a catastrophic change at the beginning of human history (primal battle) seems inconsistent with the conclusions that can be drawn from the observations of apes and monkeys" (Róheim 1934, 190). Methodologically, it was sufficient "to derive culture, i.e., all those features of our mental make-up which distinguish us from animals, from the traumata of the infancy period" (p. 197). In a posthumously published work, Róheim went still further and derived the primal horde from the Oedipus complex: "The Oedipus complex is not a "survival" of the primal-horde but, on the contrary, the primal-horde itself is to be regarded as an early form of social organization arising from the eternally human Oedipus complex" (Róheim 1972, 108).

THE GENITALITY OF MYTHS

In abandoning Freud's speculations about prehistory in favor of observations of child development in living cultures, Róheim adopted a point of view that permitted the specificity of myth to become increasingly visible. To tell us, as Freud (1913) did, that myth, ritual, totemism, religion, and magic all stem from the Oedipus complex is to tell us nothing that is distinctive of myth. However, Róheim (1934) noted that "the peculiarity" of myths "is not that they can be analytically interpreted as more or less distorted representations of the Oedipus situation." The whole of culture can be interpreted in such a fashion. Rather, myths "describe the conflict between the one and the many, between the super-man and humanity. Moreover, they are often concerned with some decisive change, such as the origin of civilization or of a particular culture, that is associated with their tragedy" (pp. 159–60). Róheim had noticed as early as 1925 that some myths were exceptions to Freud's theory of the return of the repressed:

> In analysing Central Australian myths we have found that the actions which lead to human and animal multiplication are unconscious, symbolic equivalents of coitus; here [in a Torres Straits myth] we find the open statement that it was coitus which made the food-plants grow.... it is Australia which has conserved the repressed and Torres Straits which possess the unrepressed forms. What is quite conscious in the north is merely symbolic in the south. (Róheim 1925, 323)

In 1934, Róheim added that cultural conventions regarding symbolism are operative in myths and must be taken into account by their interpreters:

> The myth is only comprehensible to those who understand its technical language. According to the fundamental rule in all Central Australian myths the hunter and the hunted correspond; kangaroo people feed on kangaroo meat, wallaby people on wallabies, etc. I assume therefore that the Mountain-dove ancestors are also kangaroos. (Róheim 1934, 162)

These several observations were inconsistent with a psychoanalytic theory, such as Rank's, that treated myth as a spontaneous manifestation of the unconscious that was symptomatic of a cultural neurosis. Myths involve the relations between the leader and the led. They concern the origin of cultural institutions, and they deploy symbols in manners that are consistent with conventional, consciously understood meanings in their cultures of origin. On the other hand, in an analysis of the Northwest Coast Indian myth "Raven Releases the Sun," Róheim (1948, 315) found that "the myth operates like a dream with a repetition of symbolic contents."

Róheim noticed an additional specificity in an article on "The Dragon and the Hero" (1940a). Discussing the Hindu myth of the sky god Indra's defeat of the dragon Vrtra, Róheim interpreted the basic theme in Kleinian terms as a preoedipal child's relation to his mother. "The hero god Indra represents the body destruction phantasy of the infant who wishes to cleave or pierce his mother's body and tears out the good objects it contains" (Róheim 1940a, 44–45). Róheim also drew attention to "the transformation of the original theme" that occurred as the myth progressed:

> The transformation is not only in the secondary elaboration, that is in the share of the Ego in the development of the myth. This is one part of the process of course. It results in the increasing elaboration of the narrative; the story is longer, there is more art in it, and it is not so easy to recognize the original phantasy material. The other factor of transformation is in the Id. The phantasy content "grows up" through a gradual genitalisation which overlaps body destruction phantasy material. (pp. 60–61)

Róheim observed that the psychosexual materials at the beginning of the myths were not the same unconscious topics as those at the end. The tale began by symbolizing infantile concerns, but it narrated increasingly mature concerns as the story progressed. Corroborating his finding, Róheim discussed a similarly developmental progression in the Greek myth of Athena. "In all her other activities excepting war, she represents reparation, or at any rate the opposite of body destruction" (p. 70). In their cumulative effect, the myths of Athena trace "the development of the goddess from body destruction through anxiety to sublimation" (p. 71). Róheim summarized: "Besides this transformation of the original phantasy content due to defense mechanisms there is also an Id-transformation ... new latent contents are expressed in the same phantasy frame. Like an individual, the myth grows up" (p. 88).

Róheim (1945) termed myths that symbolize unconscious development as *mythes de passage*, or transition myths:

> The period of life which conditions the transition from mother to wife, from old to new love object, is dramatized: *the penis becomes the hero of this drama*. It is subject to operations, it is represented in symbols. The boys hear and see the story of the wandering phallic ancestors and they themselves become wanderers in space and time.... The mythological material helps the young men to grow up, and to make the transition from the Oedipus situation to marriage.... The essential theme is the relation of the individual to the object-world, and libidinal cathexis as the defense used by human beings to bear the deprivations of object loss or separation.... It represents the wanderings of human beings from the cradle to the grave in a web of daydreams. It represents our efforts to deal with the problem of growing up, aided by the illusion of an eternal future. (Róheim 1945, 16, 17, 249)

Róheim's suggestion that identification with the myths assists children to mature was the beginning of a significant revision of the diagnostic implication of mythology. Ferenczi (1933) had proposed that for men coitus represents a re-entrance within, and so a regression to the womb. A symbol of returning to the womb might express a wish to flee life and return to a fetal state, but it might instead be used to express an unconscious wish for healthy adult coitus. Ferenczi's proposal was immediately accepted, because it is consistent with common clinical experience. No one mentioned, however, that it was inconsistent with Freud's (1900) contention that only the repressed undergoes symbolization. Why should healthy ideas, that are able to be conscious, undergo symbolic representation? For Róheim, it sufficed that Ferenczi's theory changed the diagnostic climate so that he was able to discuss symbols of coitus in terms of wholesome adult genitality rather than unresolved Oedipal fixations.

Róheim also faced up to the theoretic puzzle. Abraham's approach to myths as dreams remained his point of departure. Once more, it was the implications of Abraham's technique that intrigued Róheim. Granting that myths can be interpreted as though they were dreams, how are myths like dreams, and how do they differ? What are the theoretic implications of the various points of comparison and contrast?

"In various Australian languages, we find identical or similar words for dream, the mythical past, and ancestors. Are these narratives based on dreams? or how are we to interpret this identity of names?" (Róheim 1945, 6).

To account for their symbolization of ideas that are not repressed, Róheim likened myths to daydreams:

> Perhaps rites and religion are not based on dreams but are somehow related to dreams, or more exactly, to day-dreams.... This means simply that somebody in the past with an urge to communicate, first told a daydream, probably interwoven with real dream elements. Generations have been reelaborating this story in fantasy, and generations have been rehistoricizing these fantasy products in actual practice. (Róheim 1945, 7)

Over the years, Róheim became increasingly convinced of his proposal:

> I have found that many myths are based on dreams actually dreamed and retold. This dream origin becomes very probable if somebody — one of the *dramatis personae* — is asleep while the action continues. Moreover, the hypnagogic phantasy continues in the dream and the hypnagogic phantasy is usually one of falling into a cave, lake, and so forth, i.e., going back into the womb.... or coitus with the mother. (Róheim 1951, 185–86)

In *The Gates of the Dream* (1952), Róheim developed these concepts into a general theory of dreams and myths. He began by linking the dream to Ferenczi's theory of genitality:

> The dream is primarily a reaction to the fact that we are asleep, or to put it differently, there is such a thing as a basic dream which represents this reaction. Other layers are then added to the dream and these are derived from our waking life....
> Freud writes:
> "Sleep is a reactivation of the intrauterine situation. We have rest, warmth, and absence of stimuli, many people even sleep in the fetal position." (Róheim 1952, 1)

Róheim summarized that "the basic dream represents both regression into the womb and coitus" (p. 94). "The dream image is essentially genital (phallic)" (p. 116). Róheim allowed, however, for an overlay. "The dream is also conditioned by conflicts or wishes of waking life.

Oral aggression and talion anxiety or the primal scene are subjects of the dream but not derived from dreaming" (p. 195).

Armed with a theory of the basic dream, Róheim next addressed the presence of equivalent symbolism in some myths:

> Mythical images are in caves because they are dream images and the dream, or rather sleep, represents a regression into the womb. (Róheim 1952, 113)

> The shaman's initiation and his shamanistic activity frequently follow the same pattern. I believe we can use this analogy here, the journey to the other world, or the world under the ground, or the cave is really a journey into the mother, *the basic dream*. (p. 228)

> If the medicine man's flight is an erection and the goal of this flight a phenomenon in nature that represents the primal scene, the latent content of the dream is evidently the sexual desire of the child as witness of the primal scene. (p. 241)

To account for the resemblances of the basic dream and many myths, Róheim suggested that the one inspires the other. "I would assume that most of the stories, myths, etc., were based on dreams, and the others, freely invented because the dream stories were already being told and thus stimulated fantasy" (p. 401; For an extended discussion, see Morales 1988.):

> The core of the myth is a dream actually dreamed once upon a time by one person. Told and retold it became a myth, a creed even, and gave rise to gods or philosophies because it appealed to those who heard it. All had dreamed something similar; some had remembered these dreams, some had repressed them. What follows is history. How cultural influences spread from one people to another and are accepted is beyond the scope of this book. However, the unconscious somehow "knows" the dream origin of the myth. Here and there it would crop up in varying forms. (p. 428)

Róheim regarded his theory of the basic dream as a complement to his theory of transitional myths. "In general I suspect that there are two sources of mythology. The dream is the one we are discussing in this book, the other would be the problem of growing up" (p. 401).

In a posthumously published book on *Hungarian and Vogul Mythology* (1954), Róheim offered yet another interpretation of the genitality in myths. "The nucleus of all these beliefs and myths is the primal scene, or rather a dream of the primal scene" (p. 67). Whether coitus symbolism represented a regression to the womb, or a fantasy of parental coitus (the primal scene), or the Oedipus complex, both the basic dream and a large class of myths manifested unconscious fantasies of coitus. Róheim (1972) summarized: "*Myth is created by the individual:* the group only rewrites it, modifies it, etc.: first taking shape in the form of a dream, the myth reflects a conflict in the development of every individual — that of growing up; hence the hero of the story is genital libido" (p. 220).

Róheim avoided use of the phrase unconscious fantasy, presumably to distance himself from Kleinian formulations. Like Klein, Róheim developed Ferenczi's theory of unconscious genitality into a theory of universal, unconscious fantasizing; but he made no use of Klein's theories of internalized objects.

CONCLUDING REFLECTIONS

Psychoanalytic studies of the art, literature, culture, mythology, religion, politics, and so forth were originally termed applied psychoanalysis because clinicians regarded them as applications of clinical theories to extraclinical data. In this manner, the symbolism of typical dreams was applied to the interpretation of myths. For Freud and his original coworkers, applied psychoanalysis served the purpose of popularizing psychoanalysis for a mass audience through writings on topics of general interest and appeal. The procedure was problematic, however, on two important counts. The technique of applied psychoanalysis assumes that theories that are based on pathological phenomena encountered in clinical contexts can validly be exported to cultural phenomena in the absence of any evidence of morbidity. It also assumes that cultural phenomena lack the integrity to merit the construction of original theories on the basis of their evidence. The professionalization of applied psychoanalysis, its transformation from amateur studies by clinicians into interdisciplinary areas of study that meet professional standards in both contributing disciplines (Devereux 1957), began with Róheim's work in psychoanalytic anthropology.

In the area of myth, Róheim's contributions were fundamental. He replaced Freud's incoherent speculations about the primal horde with a methodologically tenable concern with child development. He insisted on a universal biological basis to the human psyche, but also on a conventional, historical approach to any given culture's symbolism. He brilliantly recognized that distinctive child-rearing techniques in different cultures each produce distinctive culturally shared traumas, the consequences of which may be found in myth and other symbolic phenomena. He noticed that some myths symbolize developmental progress, and he attempted (not fully persuasively) to validate Abraham's method of interpreting myths as though they were dreams by applying Ferenczi's theory of genitality to both dreams and myths.

4

MYTH AS DEFENSE AND ADAPTATION

The classical approach to myth addressed the puzzle of myths' irrationality. The first psychoanalytic writers established that the manner in which myths are irrational is the same manner by which dreams are irrational. Jones (1931) soon cautioned, however, that "one can no longer — as writers have often done — regard the problem as solved as soon as one has simply noted the similarity between dreams and certain myths" (p. 66). Myths use symbols in ways similar to dreams to express similar unconscious concerns. However, given the aversion for psychoanalysis among most anthropologists and folklorists, these basic insights were dissociated from the main body of scholarship on myths. The Culture and Personality school within American anthropology found it necessary again and again to provide introductory lessons on psychoanalysis to other social scientists. Anthropologists as late as Melville Jacobs (1952) and Victor Barnouw (1955) continued to go to the trouble of demonstrating in detail the cross-cultural validity of Freud's (1905) extension of the concept of sexuality to include oral, anal, and Oedipal manifestations in addition to genitality.

Exploration of the differences between myths and dreams was initially a secondary concern. Myths are consciously told. They are publicly shared. If their symbols compare with the symbols in dreams, their cultural position places them in a category apart. Why do most of the world's cultures not only tolerate but venerate irrational, dream-like stories? What is the basis for myths' authority? Why are myths believed to be true, when folktales are regarded as fictions?

In keeping with the general tendency in psychoanalysis for phenomenological observations to proceed in advance of theoretic language that is able to make sense of the observations, the psychological function of myths was perceived fairly clearly, long before appropriate formulations were introduced. Malinowski (1926) had placed functionalism on the agenda:

> The really important thing about the myth is its character of a retrospective, ever-present, live actuality. It is to the native neither a fictitious story, nor an account of a dead past; it is a statement of a bigger reality still partially alive. It is alive in that its precedent, its law, its moral, still rule the social life of the natives. (p. 127)

Psychoanalysts were aware of the validity of Malinowski's observation long before they could conceptualize the manifest impact of myth in meaningful psychological terms. Appropriate formulations were not possible for classical psychoanalysts but instead awaited the paradigm shift from libido theory to ego psychology (La Barre 1948; Dundes 1987, 3–46).

ABRAM KARDINER

Anthropologists credit the psychoanalyst Abram Kardiner (1891 to 1981) and the anthropologist Ralph Linton (1893 to 1953) with the "basic personality structure approach" to culture. Kardiner did not achieve a comparable reputation among psychoanalysts because his formulations were considered unorthodox. Kardiner's background was multidisciplinary. He had medical training, did graduate studies in anthropology with Franz Boas, and received a didactic analysis from Freud. Because Róheim deserves credit for the theory that culturally typical child-rearing shapes culturally typical personality traits, Kardiner and Linton are better regarded as the authors of an ego psychological approach to anthropology, including mythology. Although Kardiner had been analyzed by Freud and was a training psychoanalyst at the New York Psychoanalytic Institute, his views on culture were criticized for their proximity to the cultural approach of Erich Fromm, Karen Horney, and others. Like Fromm and Horney, Kardiner rejected the universality of the Oedipus complex; and the psychoanalytic politics of the 1930s and 1940s has long skewed the evaluation of Kardiner's work.

The Culture and Personality school of American anthropology had its origin in the personal friendship of the ethnolinguist Edward Sapir and Harry Stack Sullivan, the founder of interpersonal psychiatry. Franz Boas would send his graduate students in anthropology at Columbia University to Sapir at Yale University to learn Native American languages, and Sapir would recommend both personal psychoanalyses and psychoanalytic orientations in their anthropological research. More than anyone else, however, Kardiner created an interdisciplinary community of clinical psychoanalysts and professional anthropologists. Out of the interdisciplinary seminars that Kardiner pioneered at Columbia University came the American Psychoanalytic Association's single longest-lived colloquium, the Interdisciplinary Colloquium on Psychoanalytic Questions and Methods in Anthropological Fieldwork. Many of the Colloquium's participants contributed to the nineteen volumes of *The Psychoanalytic Study of Society*. The unprecedented success of Kardiner's outreach inevitably came at a considerable intellectual price. His concessions to the consensus in anthropology led him to theoretic formulations in psychoanalysis that may most kindly be described as mediocre. To characterize them as unorthodox or neo-Freudian is to miscomprehend their place in psychoanalytic history. Nearly forty years were to elapse before conversations in the community founded by Kardiner were to articulate a methodology that satisfied both anthropologists and psychoanalysts. It is unreasonable to expect Kardiner to have bridged the whole of the interdisciplinary gap on his own.

As early as 1933, Kardiner recognized that Freud's claims about the universality of orality, anality, genitality, and their sequential developments could be tested through examinations of cross-cultural evidence (Kardiner 1956, 59). His attention was early drawn to Egyptian, Greek, and biblical stories. In 1937, he examined some legends from the Marquesa Islands in Polynesia:

> Here there was also a collection of family constellation tales: the father-daughter stories, which were like those we know, but without punishment; and mother-son stories that were radically different. The woman is called evil, she pursues the innocent little boy, forces him into sex activity on threat of being devoured. Why are these stories so different from those in Western culture? (Kardiner 1956, 60–61)

To account for cultural variation in the family dynamics that are portrayed in myths, Kardiner introduced culture as an independent variable in psychoanalytic theorizing. Classical analysts had always treated culture as a dependent variable. Cultural items were conscious manifestations of instincts. Whether the cultural items were healthy sublimations or symptoms of morbidity, in neither event were they independent of instincts. In *The Individual and His Society* (Kardiner 1939), he characterized the classical position as follows:

> One viewpoint takes the position that man is phylogenetically endowed with certain drives or "instincts" which press for satisfaction through objects in the outer world; that these "instincts," in the course of their ontogenesis, go through certain phylogenetically predetermined and regularly repeated phases of development, at each of which an arrest of development may take place; and that, in some way as yet unknown, institutional systems are derived from these "instincts" and their derivatives according to the extent of their development.... this situation is viewed not as an encounter with institutions, but as an unconscious hereditary constellation which acts as the prime mover of the regressive adaptation. The institutions of a culture, from this point of view, are adventitious excrescences consequent upon certain drives seeking for expression, and hence quite meaningless as influences on human nature. (p. 16)

Finding the classical position overly simplistic, Kardiner treated cultural institutions as independent variables:

> The other viewpoint, the validity of which we shall attempt to establish, is that the individual stands midway between institutions which mold and direct his adaptation to the outer world, and his biological needs, which press for gratification. This viewpoint places a heavy emphasis on institutions and stresses the significant role they play in creating the adaptive systems of the individual. The institutions in this view can be identified and their effects on the individual traced. But the coördinates against which all these effects are charted are the basic biologically determined needs of man. (p. 17)

Because Kardiner was offering a general theory of culture that emphasized its social institutions, he discussed myths only briefly. His main point was that myths constitute a social institution that contributes to the shaping of individual personalities. "Myths have a functional relationship to the social organization, and when their usefulness is exhausted, they are changed" (p. 103). Myths "are commentaries on current social organizations, and demonstrate attending conflicts" (p. 104). If one were to define Aranda women's custom of sleeping on top of their children as a cultural institution, Róheim's view of cultural variation would be accurately expressed by Kardiner's (1939) formulation: "The thing transmitted is the primary institution; the fantasies resulting from the pressures created by these institutions on the individual do not need to be inherited. Each individual can create them afresh" (p. 107).

Róheim (1940b, 529) remarked, however, that "I had a curious reaction when I first pondered this theory. I felt rather like the proverbial absent-minded professor who does not recognize his own child when by chance he meets him." He generously acknowledged that "Kardiner has developed what was little more than a hint in my publications into a systematic theory of *basic personality*" (Róheim 1947, 29). At the same time, Róheim took sharp exception to Kardiner's treatment of culture as an independent variable. In Róheim's view, Kardiner had left the biological basis of psychoanalysis for a sociological approach akin to that of Erich Fromm:

> Kardiner's book is an attempt to base psychoanalysis on sociology.... the very corner stones of the psychoanalytic structure disappear and we have Fromm instead of Freud. The most important function of the family is that it becomes the instrument for forging the socially acceptable character. The father is not the prototype (*Vorbild*) of social authority but its replica (*Abbild*).... A psychoanalytic ego psychology must be based on the concept of conflict between id, ego and superego. In Kardiner's scheme this conflict is eliminated. It is replaced by the conflict between the individual and society. (Róheim 1940b, 528, 530, 531)

Kardiner agreed with Fromm and the majority approach to cultural relativism in anthropology when he trivialized the Oedipus complex as a response to "a specific type of patriarchal family organization, operating on a given biological make-up of man" (Kardiner 1939, 100). Fromm's (1944) formulation was more explicitly Marxist. He suggested:

> that the Oedipus complex be interpreted not as a result of the child's sexual rivalry with the parent of the same sex but as the child's fight with irrational authority represented by the

> parents ... the emphasis is not on the incestuous wishes of the child and their necessarily tragic outcome, its original sin, but on the parents' prohibitive influence on the normal sexual activity of the child. (p. 410)

In their utopianism, both Kardiner and Fromm missed Freud's point that the "biological make-up of man" (Kardiner) or "normal sexual activity of the child" (Fromm) is inherently conflicted. The Oedipus complex was Freud's attempt to formulate his basic insight that we, as social beings, are necessarily at odds with the asocial impulses of our biological natures. It matters little to psychoanalysts whether myths are explained in terms of the triadic Oedipus complex (Reik 1921; Flügel 1924) or tales of mother goddesses are interpreted in terms of the pre-Oedipal mother-infant dyad, in which mothers both excite and terrify sexually (Weigert-Vowinkel 1938; Brenner 1950). Whatever variations may occur in the manifest organization of cultures and their myths, ego psychologists understood the unconscious to be divided against itself. Psychic conflict was not identified, as it had been prior to Freud's (1923a) structural hypothesis, with an alleged repression of the unconscious by consciousness. Because psychic conflict cannot be ended through submission to the unconscious, psychic conflict was now located in the unconscious.

In the late 1930s and early 1940s, Kardiner participated in an interdisciplinary seminar of psychoanalysts and anthropologists at Columbia University. One result was a multiauthored book, *The Psychological Frontiers of Society*, published in 1945 and signed by Kardiner together with the anthropologists Ralph Linton, Cora Du Bois, and James West. The joint publication was in some ways a more classical formulation than Kardiner's solo outing of 1939 had been. In some of Kardiner's 1945 phrasings, cultural institutions were implied to be dependent variables. "As the experiences varied, so did the products of the projective systems in folklore and religion" (p. 23). "If we know how the basic personality is established, we can make certain predictions about the institutions this personality is likely to invent" (p. 29).

An additional product of Kardiner's conversations with anthropologists was his adoption of anthropologist A. R. Radcliffe-Brown's model of social functionalism, with its unearned assumption of social homeostasis. Kardiner (1956) wrote: "Human relations are shaped, directed, restricted, permitted, emphasized or underplayed according to a plan that may be called the homeostatic pattern of the society as a whole. This homeostatic pattern is one that permits cooperation and survival of the group" (p. 64).

Functionalism had been introduced in the study of myth by Malinowski. Rejecting nineteenth-century theories that myths are allegories of the sun, moon, or weather (Dorson 1955), Malinowski ignored myths' meanings and instead drew attention to their living functions in cultures that relate them. Myths function, in Malinowski's (1926, 101) famous metaphor, as a "pragmatic charter of primitive faith and moral wisdom." Malinowski had regarded the functions of cultural institutions to be various. Radcliffe-Brown instead assumed that social institutions function to produce and maintain cultures. The assumption is not only unearned but improbable. Cultures are not self-regulating homeostatic entities. Cultures rise and fall. They grow, expand, exploit, war on their neighbors, sicken, wane, atrophy, suffer defeat, and are destroyed.

Importantly, there was a gap between Kardiner's claims and Róheim's description of Kardiner's results. Kardiner claimed to be treating biological inheritance and social institutions as independent variables. Did he actually do so? Róheim criticized Kardiner for replacing instinct theory with sociology. Who was right? Consider the following explanation of cultural relativism by Kardiner (1956):

> Man always acts in accordance with what he *deems* rational. What is rational at one time becomes irrational at another. In the Old Testament there is evidence of the alteration of custom. At one time, it was in accordance with reason to sacrifice children to the deity for public security. The same practice, two hundred years later, is considered irrational or barbarous. We know that the Phoenicians were practicing child sacrifice at the time of the Punic Wars, while the same practice was abandoned by the Hebrews (sacrifice of Isaac by Abraham) a thousand years before. (p. 66)

Kardiner did not discuss the implications of his statement. Is cultural relativism a legitimate standard for the evaluation of mental health? Is mental health in each culture to be adjudicated on the culture's own criteria? Was it wholesome to sacrifice children in early Israel, as also among the Phoenicians a millennium later, because they each thought it was; but pathological to do so in later Israel, because the Israelites had come to consider it sinful? Kardiner's oversight is all the more troubling because his two major books were published at the beginning and end of the Hitlerian War. Was he unaware that his theories provided an apologetic for Nazism?

Devereux took immediate and repeated issue with the promotion of cultural relativism in psychoanalysis. In an article on "Maladjustment and Social Neurosis," Devereux (1939) complained of

> the widespread confusion between neurosis and maladjustment. Psychiatrists as well as social scientists are both responsible for this confusion. Having realized that certain so-called neurotic, or even psychotic, phenomena are socially acceptable and sometimes even at a premium in various primitive societies, they have hastened to conclude — at least implicitly — that neurosis and maladjustment are interchangeable and coextensive terms. (p. 844)

Devereux did not name Kardiner, but it was Kardiner's replacement of biology with sociology that produced the confusion that Devereux sought to clarify.

In an article on "Normal and Abnormal: The Key Concepts of Ethnopsychiatry," Devereux (1970) returned to the topic of cultural relativism with devastating satire:

> This approach reduces diagnosis to a determination of degrees of adjustment. It leads one to say that in April, 1945 a German psychiatrist's task was completed the day his patient joined the Nazi party, while in May, 1945 it was finished the day the patient joined, in Frankfurt am Main, the Christian-Democratic party, or, in Frankfurt an der Oder, the Communist party. This theory disregards the fact that a society can be so 'sick' that only abnormal people can adjust to it. (p. 114)

Devereux (1958, 365) concluded, "Not adjustment, which is static, but the capacity for creative readjustment is the real criterion of sanity."

Although Kardiner's brand of cultural relativism retains followers, his enduring contribution to psychoanalytic anthropology remains his effort, as he conceived it, to shift the discussion from libido theory to ego psychology (Kardiner 1959, 88). Freud understood people to be dominated by self-interest in the service of sexuality and aggression. The self-interest was optimally rational, but it often was not. In *Civilization and Its Discontents*, Freud (1930) suggested that culture is internalized in the superego as a means to control instinctual self-interest sufficiently to enable people to live together more or less harmoniously in social groupings. Kardiner took exception to this formulation. "Psychoanalysis is responsible for the fiction, promulgated largely by Freud, that culture is predominantly restrictive; the reverse is true. It is predominantly directive" (Kardiner 1959, 102).

To account for the adaptive aspects of culture, Kardiner ignored Freud's remarks about the superego and instead drew attention to Anna Freud's model of the ego. "[Freud's] daughter Anna rediscovered the adaptive devices described by her father in 1900, but which since that time had enjoyed a position that was extraterritorial to the theory. They were now called mechanisms of defense" (Kardiner 1959, 87).

THE MECHANISMS OF DEFENSE

Where classical psychoanalysis was concerned, above all, with unconscious sexuality and aggression, psychoanalytic ego psychology is distinguished by the priority that it assigns to the ego's management of instinct-derivatives. The clinical practice of ego psychology begins with a long phase of defense analysis, which addresses the patient's defense mechanisms, before deep interpretations of unconscious sexuality and aggression are offered. By contrast, Kleinian object relations theory perpetuated the procedure of classical psychoanalysis to offer deep interpretations early and frequently.

Ego psychology had its foundations in Freud's writings of the 1920s, but first became a distinctive approach to psychoanalysis in the 1930s. In *Inhibitions, Symptoms, and Anxiety*, Freud (1926a) listed ten manners by which the ego defends itself against dangerous thoughts: regression, reaction-formation, isolation, undoing, repression, introjection or identification, projection, turning against the self, reversal, and sublimation or displacement of instinctual aims. To this list of defenses, Anna Freud (1966) added identification with the aggressor (pp. 116–120). The list has since continued to grow.

For Freud, *das Ich*, "the I," was a metaphor that signified the part of the mind with which a person consciously identifies. In a loose sense, it was Freud's way of discussing the self. More technically, however, he defined the ego as the part of the mind that performs rational thinking, the type of thought that he considered a "secondary process." Freud's (1923a, 1940b) concept of the ego did not include the defense mechanisms that Anna Freud (1966) attributed to it. Freud (1926a) explained:

> Symptom-formation... has two assets: one, hidden from view, brings about the alteration in the id in virtue of which the ego

> is removed from danger; the other, presented openly, shows what has been created in place of the instinctual process that has been affected — namely, the substitutive formation.
>
> It would, however, be more correct to ascribe to the *defensive process* what we have just said about symptom-formation and to use the latter term as synonymous with substitute-formation. (p. 145)

In this formulation, defense consists of (1) unconscious stimulus barriers, such as repression, that enlarge the dynamic unconscious repressed and so remove the ego from danger, and (2) the substitution of a fantasy for the repressed that manifests the repressed in symbolic fashion. The stimulus barriers are ego functions, and they alone are truly defensive. The substitute-formations are not ego functions; they are products of unconscious symbol-formation. Freud (1926a) explained them as pathological symptoms to which the ego makes an accommodation:

> It is ... only natural that the ego should try to prevent symptoms from remaining isolated in one way or another, and to incorporate them into its organization.... The ego now proceeds to behave as though it recognized that the symptom had come to stay and that the only thing to do was to accept the situation in good part and draw as much advantage from it as possible. It makes an adaptation to the symptom — to this piece of the internal world which is alien to it — just as it normally does to the real external world. (pp. 98–99)

Freud's (1926a) notion of defense mechanisms as "a kind of frontier-station with a mixed garrison" (p. 99) reflects the complexity of their origin. Every so-called defense mechanism combines a stimulus barrier, belonging to the ego, with a fantasy formation, of unconscious origin, to which the ego has adapted. Why does the ego accommodate selected pathological symptoms? Were the unconscious to be constantly producing new symptoms, the ego would be obliged to respond to them all, resulting in unwanted and frequent mood swings. Instituting selected symptoms as permanent structures does not lessen their irrationality. It has the advantage, however, of making the type of irrationality predictable. Because the predictability provides the ego with stability that is necessary for mood regulation, the automatization of selected symptoms may reasonably be regarded as a kind of defense.

Unfortunately, Freud failed to distinguish clearly between stimulus barriers and the symptoms that the ego automatizes for its purposes of stability. The oversight led to the widespread neglect of the origin and nature of the automatized symptoms. Anna Freud's *The Ego and the Mechanisms of Defense* (1966), first published in 1936, expressed an over-simplification that went unchallenged for half a century. Anna Freud (1966, 157) postulated "the ego's primary antagonism to instinct — its dread of the strength of the instincts" (p. 157). She maintained her position throughout her life. "Many disputed it when I said it, and I still say that the ego as such is hostile rather than friendly and helpful to the instincts, because it's against its nature to be friendly" (Sandler with Freud 1985, 494).

Anna Freud's concept of defense flowed similarly from her failure to embrace the subtleties of her father's formulation of psychic structure. Anna Freud wrote:

> The part played by the ego in the formation of those compromises which we call symptoms consists in the unvarying use of a special method of defense, when confronted with a particular instinctual demand, and the repetition of exactly the same procedure every time that demand recurs in its stereotyped form. (p. 34)

In this presentation, defenses belong exclusively to the ego and are not themselves compromise formations. Symptoms and defenses are mutually exclusive; and it is symptoms that are compromise formations — between the instincts and the defenses! Anna Freud's account of defenses agreed with her father's formulation in so far as stimulus barriers were intended, but it misrepresented the circumstances of such defenses as regression, reaction-formation, undoing, introjection or identification, projection, turning against the self, and reversal. In her father's view, these defenses were themselves pathological symptoms.

Anna Freud's hypothesis of "the ego's primary antagonism to instinct" was able to command the devotion of ego psychologists presumably because Freud's structural concepts of id and ego were understood, for clinical purposes, on the topographic model of the old systems Unconscious and Perception-Consciousness. Anna Freud stated that for many decades she and many other psychoanalysts used both the topographic and the structural models of the mind in alternation, depending on whether, for example, they were momentarily concerned with dreams or defense mechanisms. "I definitely belong to the people who feel free to fall back on the topographical aspects whenever convenient, and to leave them aside and to speak purely structurally when that is convenient" (Sandler with A. Freud 1985, 31). In similar fashions, Bertram D. Lewin (1952), Jacob A. Arlow and Charles Brenner (1964), and Heinz Kohut (1984) estimated that most of their contemporaries reverted to the topographic hypothesis when conceptualizing dreams. I suggest that many thought in topographic terms even when they employed ego psychological terminology. Bernard Apfelbaum (1966) drew attention to the distinction I have emphasized between Freud's view of the ego as the secondary process and Anna Freud's expansion of the ego to include character defenses:

> A distinction must be drawn between two conceptions of the ego: what may be called the "reality ego" versus the "defence ego." The "reality ego" emphasizes the ego's temporizing, compromising function — as a busy mediator between the demands of reality and of the drives. The "defence ego" is a more active principle, having superordinate goals of its own, before which both reality and the drives must yield. (p. 462)

Ego psychology's transformation of the ego from a "reality ego" that performs rational thought, into a "defense ego" that includes the "character armor" (Reich 1949) of irrational defenses, depended on equating the ego with the sense of self. This step, taken within American ego psychology, later served as a point of departure for Heinz Kohut (1971, 1977, 1984), whose system of self-psychology may be seen as both a valuable contribution and an inappropriate expansion of defense analysis into a complete program of psychotherapy.

Continuing David Rapaport's (1960, 1967) project of introducing academic methodology and systematizing within ego psychology, Roy Schafer (1968) took issue with the "traces of the machine analogy in the prevailing conception of defence mechanisms" (p. 52). There are no machines in the mind. There are only thoughts. The notion of a mechanism is either a fallacy or a metaphor that refers summarily to both "the instinctual act and the defence against it" (p. 54). Morris Eagle (1984) added that "the supposition that the intensity of the instincts is threatening to the ego" derives from a reification of the metaphor of psychic energy. It is a purely fictitious notion. "The idea that instinctual impulses, particularly those of great intensity, are *inherently* dangerous to the ego derives from an *a priori* tension-reduction model of human behavior and a conception of the nervous system as naturally and ideally quiescent, and disturbed, in varying degrees, by excitation" (p. 111). Because too much energy will shatter or burn out a machine, reifying the metaphors of psychic energy and psychic structures leads to the idea that the structures of the psychical apparatus are inherently and necessarily threatened by psychic energies.

In "Analysis Terminable and Interminable," Freud (1937) corrected his daughter's formulation without naming her explicitly. He asserted that "id and ego are originally one" and "the psychical apparatus is intolerant of unpleasure" — implicitly, of unpleasure alone (pp. 240, 237). He also emphasized that defense mechanisms and symptoms are two ways of discussing the same psychic elements:

> The mechanisms of defence serve the purpose of keeping off dangers. It cannot be disputed that they are successful in this; and it is doubtful whether the ego could do without them altogether during its development. But it is also certain that they may become dangers themselves … these mechanisms are not relinquished after they have assisted the ego during the difficult years of its development….
>
> They become regular modes of reaction of his character, which are repeated throughout his life whenever a situation occurs that is similar to the original one. This turns them into infantilisms…. The adult's ego, with its increased strength, continues to defend itself against dangers which no longer exist in reality; indeed, it finds itself compelled to seek out those situations in reality which can serve as an approximate substitute for the original danger, so as to be able to justify, in relation to them, its maintaining its habitual modes of reaction. Thus we can easily understand how the defensive mechanisms, by bringing about an ever more extensive alienation from the external world and a permanent weakening of the ego, pave the way for, and encourage, the outbreak of neurosis. (pp. 237–38)

Freud here took for granted his previous account of the origin of defense mechanisms as amalgams of stimulus barriers and symptoms. Defenses can alienate the secondary process from the external world only because symptoms are among their components. As flights from reality, symptoms are inconsistent with the reality principle of secondary process thought.

Anna Freud's misunderstanding of her father's theory of defense was one of several developments in the 1930s that collectively accomplished a paradigm shift in psychoanalytic theory and technique. Wilhelm Reich's *Character Analysis* (1948), first published in 1933, emphasized that differences in character types reflected differences among the defense mechanisms that individuals favored. Ernst Kris (1934) introduced the concept of "ego-directed regression," or "regression in the service of the ego," which permitted unconscious manifestations such as play and creativity to be diagnosed as wholesome, where their classical descriptions as "regression" had meant that they were pathological. Kris's revalorization of fantasy anticipated Anna Freud's revalorization of defense mechanisms. Her catalog of defenses, first published in 1936, supported the clinical technique of defense analysis, where interpretations are made of the defenses, and efforts to interpret the unconscious drives are postponed until a later phase of the treatment. Heinz Hartmann's (1939) emphasis on the ego's devotion to adaptation completed the basic paradigm of ego psychology. Where classical psychoanalysts thought of the benefits derived from symptoms as "secondary gains" of illness, ego psychologists construed defenses as positive adaptations and left unremarked their inherently fantastic and irrational nature.

Ego psychology's revalorization of defense had immediate implications for the assessment of myth. Myths no longer had to be seen as symptoms, as Róheim had done. They could instead be treated positively as defenses. The diagnostic step was first taken by Clyde Kluckhohn (1905 to 1960), one of the last true generalists in American anthropology, who contributed to physical and sociocultural anthropology, archaeology, linguistics, and psychological anthropology. He was psychoanalyzed in 1931 to 1932, when he was occupied with graduate studies at the University of Vienna. Kluckhohn (1942) presented his view of myth as a defense in his classic article, "Myth and Rituals: A General Theory:"

> Of the ten "mechanisms of defence" which Anna Freud suggests that the ego has available, their myths and rituals afford the Navaho with institutionalized means of employing at least four. Reaction-formation has already been briefly discussed. Myths supply abundant materials for introjection and likewise (in the form of witchcraft myths) suggest an easy and culturally acceptable method of projection of hostile impulses. Finally, rituals provide ways of sublimation of aggression and

> other socially disapproved tendencies, in part, simply through giving people something to *do*.
>
> All of these "mechanisms of ego defence" will come into context only if we answer the question "adjustive with respect to what?" The existence of motivation, of "anxiety" in Navaho individuals must be accounted for by a number of different factors. In the first place — as in every society — there are those components of "anxiety," those "threats" which may be understood in terms of the "reality principle" of psychoanalysis: life *is* hard — an unseasonable temperature, a vagary of the rainfall does bring hunger or actual starvation; people *are* organically ill. In the second place, there are various forms of "neurotic" anxiety. To some extent, every society tends to have a type anxiety. In our own society it is probably sexual, although this may be true only of those segments of our society who are able to purchase economic and physical security. In most Plains Indians sexual anxiety, so far as we can tell from the available documents, was insignificant. There the basic anxiety was for life itself and for a certain quality of that life (which I cannot attempt to characterize in a few words).
>
> Among the Navaho the "type anxiety" is certainly that for health. (p. 160)

Róheim, who was later to do fieldwork with Kluckhohn among the Navajo, immediately endorsed Kluckhohn's suggestion that cultural phenomena can be viewed as defenses. Róheim (1943, 81–82) wrote: "*Defense systems against anxiety are the stuff that culture is made of* and ... specific cultures are structurally similar to specific neuroses" (Róheim's emphasis). However, Róheim always wrote of defenses with a negativity consistent with an accurate understanding of Freud's concept. Róheim (1943) described culture as a defense in that its fantasies protect us from the emotional burden of human weakness in relation to external reality. This formulation was inconsistent with an ego psychological approach that saw culture as a defense against unconscious sexuality and aggression, as though existential realities required no defenses of the psyche.

Kluckhohn's suggestion that myths function as prototypes for the formation of defense mechanisms that are typical of each culture was widely adopted by both anthropologists and psychoanalysts (Eggan 1955; La Barre 1959, 1960; Arlow 1961, 1964, 1981; Stern 1964; Skeels 1964; Ducey 1976; Boyer 1981; Boyer and Boyer 1981; Freeman

1981). Howard L. Cox (1948) provided a tidy summary of the theory of the defensive function of mythology. "Myths ... are largely projections with greater or lesser elements of wish fulfillment. They become institutionalized because they give type answers to type problems. Thus, they come to take on the nature of an anxiety allaying device" (p. 86).

In phrasing the same theory, Spiro (1951) placed a Róheimian spin on the idea of defense. "Folklore — indeed, any art form — serves at once as a projection and dissipation of some of the crucial tensions and repressed emotions of a society. Thus, motives denied external expression find an outlet in fantasy" (p. 290). Dorothy Eggan (1955) put the theory succinctly: "When a myth is congenial enough to the individual he may use it as a personal fantasy" (p. 447).

JACOB A. ARLOW

Although ego psychology was initially applied to mythology by Kardiner and reformulated in an orthodox manner by several anthropologists, beginning with Kluckhohn, clinical psychoanalysts have generally been unaware of the anthropological literature. As a result, they tend to credit Jacob A. Arlow (1912–) with the first application of ego psychology to myth. Born in New York City, Arlow is a physician and psychoanalyst. He has taught primarily at the New York Psychoanalytic Institute, but also at the New York University Psychoanalytic Institute and the Columbia University Center for Psychoanalytic Treating. He has edited *Psychoanalytic Quarterly* and served as President of the American Psychoanalytic Association (1960 to 1961). With Charles Brenner, he coauthored *Psychoanalytic Concepts and the Structural Theory* (1964), which attempted to replace the remains of classical theory, with its contrast of Consciousness and the Unconscious, with formulations that reflect the structural theory of the id, ego, and superego (Blum 1988; Kramer 1988). Arlow's major contribution to psychoanalytic theory reformulated the Kleinian concept of unconscious fantasy from an ego psychological perspective. For Arlow, unconscious fantasies are stable, organized, and pathogenic legacies of fixated, infantile traumata. Arlow's interest in unconscious fantasies extends to discussions of myths, religion, and other phenomena. Arlow's contribution to myth integrated his views on unconscious fantasies with the approach to myths developed by the Culture and Personality school in American anthropology.

Arlow (1961) began his article on "Ego Psychology and Mythology" by placing the authority of myths at the center of his exposition:

> The myth is a particular kind of communal experience. It is a special form of shared fantasy, and it serves to bring the individual into relationship with members of his cultural group on the basis of certain common needs. Accordingly, the myth can be studied from the point of view of its function in psychic integration — how it plays a role in warding off feelings of guilt and anxiety, how it constitutes a form of adaptation to reality and to the group in which the individual lives, and how it influences the crystallization of the individual identity and the formation of the superego. (p. 375)

Arlow treated myths as public expressions of communal fantasies. "Mythmakers ... take their place alongside the poets and the prophets of the community. They give words and forms to the ubiquitous fantasy wishes of mankind. They present ready-made and communally acceptable versions of wishes which heretofore were expressed in guilt-laden private fantasies" (p. 378).

The psychological functions of myths are several. Their wish-fulfillments gratify instincts; they also serve the functions of defense and adaptation. "The revision and falsification, or both, of the past and its heroes by the group serve the purpose of defense, adaptation, and instinctual gratification for the group and its individual constituents; they also serve in character building and superego formation" (p. 379).

Having related myths to private fantasies, Arlow noted that different unconscious fantasies pertain to different levels of developmental attainment:

> Fantasies are grouped around certain basic instinctual wishes, and such a group is composed of different versions or different editions of attempts to resolve the intrapsychic conflicts over these wishes. Each version corresponds to a different "psychic moment" in the history of the individual's development. It expresses the forces at play at a particular time in the person's life when the ego integrated the demands of the instinctual wishes in keeping with its growing adaptive and defensive responsibilities. (p. 377)

Because myths are appropriated as vehicles for the public expression of unconscious fantasies, variations in and among myths are appropriate to different unconscious fantasies. "Different mythological expressions on the same basic theme correspond to the different defensive editions of the unconscious fantasy in the life of the individual, externalized and artistically altered in correspondence with needs from various levels of psychic integration of the individual members of the group" (pp. 379–80).

Arlow then proceeded to analyze a variety of Greek, biblical, and American Indian myths, together with a European folktale, in illustration of his contention that myths offer a diverse range of potential solutions to unconscious conflicts (pp. 381–86). He summarized that "the mythology of a particular culture or society points the direction to the younger generation for solutions for the infantile instinctual conflicts" (p. 387).

Reverting to his original concern with the authority of myths, Arlow concluded that the models that myths provide for the solution of unconscious conflicts are cultural ideals:

> Through its mythology, the society tends to induce a climate favorable to the realization of appropriate identifications … The path is prepared for identification and subsequent character transformations in keeping with the idealized qualities of the hero. So, for example, while the little girl gets the unconscious incestuous wish fulfillment from her identification with the Madonna, she is consciously directed to the imitation of those ideal qualities of purity, virtue, and love which are represented by the Madonna. (p. 388)

In a later article on "The Madonna's Conception Through the Eyes," Arlow (1964) emphasized the religious functions of myths. "The members of a religious group share in common a gratifying unconscious wish together with a common conscious set of moral goals, and dedication to certain preferred character traits and ideals" (p. 14). To account for myths' religious functions, Arlow noted that myths have both id and superego components:

> Through unconscious identification with the central figure of the myth, the participant is afforded a certain degree of instinctual gratification. This is the id aspect of the myth which exerts its strong influence because of its wish-fulfilling nature. In myths which are central to religious tradition, as in great works of art, the superego elements ultimately must predominate. Central myths of a religion must demonstrate a high quality of sublimation and renunciation. (p. 23)

Having referred to the process of sublimation, which Freud considered wholesome, Arlow introduced a diagnostic distinction that had previously been unremarked:

> In the individual, the sublimations and character transformations which are achieved, in part, through the influence of religion may be undone by neurotic illness. In such instances the re-emergence of more primitive expressions of the unconscious instinctual wish leads to conflicts which serve as the basis for symptom formation. (p. 14)

Arlow here drew a distinction between "neurotic illness" and the sublimations and defensive functions of religions, including myths. Should the latter fail, neurotic "symptom formation" may ensue. In Arlow's formulation, the sublimations and characterological defenses of religion are implicitly not themselves neurotic.

Arlow's formulation took for granted Anna Freud's theory of defense, in which the ego and instincts are in intrinsic opposition. Health is associated with the ego's mastery of the id through its defenses; neurosis, with a regressive dominance by the id. The clinical phenomena to which Arlow pointed can also be expressed, however, in Freud's theoretical framework. When a symptom that has been stabilized and rendered automatic as a defense ceases to be stable, the innovation of other symptoms may ensue. In Freud's model of defense, there is never a question of health, but only of stable, characterological symptoms and florid, labile ones.

Arlow's orientation to mythology was both applauded and criticized. Reasserting a classical observation, Róheim's literary executor, the psychoanalyst and anthropologist Warner Muensterberger (1964), emphasized that "instinctual freedom is a major theme of the mythology of all cultures" (p. 94); but he also accepted Arlow's emphasis on ego and superego functions. "Mythology, it seems to me, helps to ward off passive or active wishes, to permit or restrain instinctual desires, largely to take the part of the superego but equally aid the ego's organizing attempts. It exercises a stabilizing influence" (p. 97).

Daniel M. A. Freeman, the current chairperson of the American Psychoanalytic Association's Interdisciplinary Colloquium on Psychoanalytic Questions and Methods in Anthropological Fieldwork, is a child psychoanalyst who has done anthropological fieldwork. Freeman (1981) suggested that single myths "contain symbolic representation of various developmental stages and conflicts" (p. 319) for both males and females:

> Different mythological expressions of the same basic theme parallel defensive structures, each deriving from corresponding stages of life, in which members of a culture attempt to resolve common intrapsychic conflicts. Shared myths derive from and represent developmental stages in the intrapsychic experience of present and past members of that culture. (p. 320)

Sidney Tarachow (1964, 11) cautioned, however, that myths can also be "maladaptive and rebellious." Harry Slochower (1970, 150) questioned, "What about the mythic hero who rebels against aspects of the social process?" Taking an optimistic view, Ducey (1979) suggested that myths both pertain to intrapsychic conflict and resolve or reduce the contradictions through the details of their narratives. "Myth serves as a cultural model for both the expression and the possible resolution of psychological conflict" (p. 73).

Diagnostic neutrality was added to Arlow's theory by L. Bryce Boyer (1916 to 2000), who blended the approaches of Róheim and ego psychology to cultural norms. Boyer was an international authority on the psychoanalysis of schizophrenia and other "deeply regressed" states. For many years he conducted fieldwork with his wife, the anthropologist Ruth M. Boyer. He edited *The Psychoanalytic Study of Society* (1981), and participated actively in the American's Interdisciplinary Colloquium. An ego psychologist by training, he was attracted to Kleinian theory through team-teaching with Thomas H. Ogden. In keeping with Freud and Róheim, rather than Anna Freud and Arlow, Boyer (1964) discussed "expressive culture" as a manifestation of the unconscious that might be defensive, but might also be otherwise. "Myths and related phenomena are group-accepted images which serve as further screening devices in the defensive and adaptive functions of the ego and reinforce suppression and repression of individual fantasies and personal myths" (p. 119).

Boyer (1977) summarized his approach to mythology in an encyclopedia article:

> Freudian psychoanalysts hold that the roots of folklore are to be found in repressed conflicts pertaining to actual individual life experiences. In their thinking, humans have a species-specific genetic heritage which, because of the unfolding of innate

traits depending on time-appropriate interaction with the intrafamilial environment, is essentially biosocial. Their developmental level at birth necessitates prolonged socialization before they can become acceptable adults in their societies. They have like basic biological and psychological needs and are subject to like frustrations and intrapsychic conflicts by their puericultural experiences. The vicissitudes of their innate drive derivatives are shaped by cultural requirements, reflected in child-rearing methods. Idiosyncratic psychological defensive techniques, including private dreams, hallucinations, and fantasies, do not suffice to quell their guilts and anxieties, conscious and unconscious. Those defensive techniques are supported by others which are supplied by expressive culture, including folklore.

The latent themes of dream and folklore are understood preconsciously and/or unconsciously by audiences to whom they are related, to the degree that listeners share and cathect the unresolved conflicts that are expressed in the related dream or myth. Children have wishes which they consider to be unacceptable to their parents. When those parents express their similar desires or do not react with disapproval to the revealed wish of the child, he feels less apprehension. The adult remains to some extent a child, and requires approval and reinforcement of individual psychological defensive maneuvers. Influential societal members, secular or religious, are used as parent surrogates. Religious superiors are more useful models for reduction of anxiety regarding the arcane. The public expression of their dreams, latent parts of which are preconsciously understood by their audience, permits adults of their community the use of those dreams, further disguised by secondary revision into items of oral literature, and thus altered in manners which make them culturally acceptable. Thus, because of this community of intrapsychic conflicts and primitive meanings of symbols and the limited number of defensive techniques available to the ego, all of which are reflected in dream motifs, identical or similar folklore items can arise at any time....

The item of oral literature which is to be included in an existent folklore stock must contain latent elements which make it suitable to serve the individual and group functions of folklore.... Whatever the reason may be that the folklore of

> one group is accepted into that of another, its latent themes and symbols must present alternate means of presenting group cohesive lessons and supporting individual defensive and adaptive techniques. (pp. 425–26)

Absent from Boyer's formulations were any references to mental health and illness. Boyer carefully balanced references to defense with references to adaptation in order to conform to Hartmann's (1939) theory that ego mechanisms that originate in the service of defense may with time and increased mental health come to be deployed in the service of adaptation.

In conversation with Muensterberger and Boyer at an Interdisciplinary Colloquium in the late 1980s, I obtained their agreement to the following implications of Boyer's formulation. If, as Róheim proposed, myths address childhood traumas that are typical products of child-rearing techniques in their cultures of origin, the existence of the myths is not necessary evidence of psychopathology. The stories are themselves diagnostically neutral. Some people respond to trauma by succumbing to mental illness. Others triumph over psychological conflicts through wholesome adaptations. Different people may use the same myths to express the divergent outcomes of their own experiences. One person may use a myth morbidly that another person uses in a wholesome way. In addition, a myth that is used defensively during one period in a life may at a later date be used in a healthy manner.

THE NAVAJO COYOTEWAY CEREMONIAL

To illustrate the ego psychological approach to myth, consider the myths and rituals of the Navajo Coyoteway ceremonial. The Navajo, together with the various Apache tribes, form the Southern Athapascan linguistic group. Resident in the United States Southwest for less than a millennium, the Navajo tribe has only in the last three centuries adopted pastoralism and agriculture from the neighboring Pueblo tribes. In the process, Pueblo-derived agricultural religion has been added to the shamanic base of Navajo hunter religion (Wyman 1975). From a comparative viewpoint (Hultkrantz 1973), a Navajo *hataali,* or Chanter, may be described as an institutionalized shaman. Women may serve as Chanters at the Kinaalda, or girl's puberty ceremonial; but Chanters at all other ceremonials are men. Because the Navajo have no rites that are not shamanic, the systematization of Navajo ceremonials on Pueblo models has transformed shamanic rites into occasions of group religion. In one survey, Kluckhohn (1938) ascertained that adult men devoted twenty-five to thirty-three percent of their waking hours to ceremonials, whereas adult women devoted fifteen to twenty percent, in both cases either as patients or as spectators. At the same time, the Navajo Chanter retains remarkably close affinities with the practices of shamans among Northern Athapascan hunter-gatherers, such as the Carrier of the British Columbia interior (Jenness 1941). His primary activity is as a healer, always of a single patient at a time. His major procedure is, in Navajo idiom, to chant, that is, to sing to the accompaniment of a rattle. The Chanter's psychological state is unremarked, whereas the patient, who is called the one sung over, undergoes profound psychological reaction by way of cure.

In Navajo thought, a Holy Person afflicts illness or causes mishap in response to a human breach of taboo: not to punish but to inform that a breach of taboo has given offense. The sufferer then consults with relatives, who in turn summon a diagnostic diviner to discover the identities of the broken taboo and the offended Holy Person. The relatives next summon a Chanter to perform the appropriate ceremonial. The Navajo had more than forty illness-specific ceremonials, each with its own specialized Chanters. Holyway ceremonials, to which class Coyoteway belongs, are commonly designed to reconcile the patient with an offended supernatural. Once reconciliation occurs, the Holy Person is mollified and has no further motive to continue signaling offense by means of affliction. Cure then results. Should a ceremonial prove ineffectual, it is assumed that the illness has been diagnosed improperly and the wrong Holy Person's ceremonial employed (Kluckhohn and Leighton, 1974; Reichard 1970).

Coyoteway was a nine-night ceremonial to cure illnesses believed to be caused by the Holy Person, Coyote. A performance of the ceremonial was recorded by Luckert (1979) shortly before the rite became extinct. Taboos surrounding Coyote were various and chiefly pertained to real animals of his species. Coyotes were not to be hurt or killed. Coyote flesh might never be eaten. In hunting, the viscera of game animals were to be left for coyotes to scavenge, as the share of game that was owed to the Holy Person, Coyote, who was man's companion in the hunt. Coyotes were not to be watched as they died, lest their twitches enter the onlooker and produce disease. Dead coyote carcasses were not to be touched. Symptoms diagnosed as Coyote illness appear to have included nervous malfunctions, mania, sex frenzy, and rabies (Luckert 1979). As will presently become clear, apart from rabies, Coyote illness proves a content-specific neurosis with attendant somatizations.

Hunter Ritualism

Like the Coyoteway ceremonial, the Navajo practice of the ritual hunt became extinct in the late twentieth century. According to Luckert (1975, 136), the Navajo conceived of the ritual hunt in terms of a "dualism of two distinct spheres, the realm of procreation and growth over against the reality of killing and death." To my understanding, the herbivorous game animals, deer, antelope, and in myth the now-scarce mountain sheep and buffalo, were classified with human female plant-gatherers. The carnivorous predatory species of wolf, bobcat, mountain lion, snake, and in myth bear and coyote, were classified with human male hunters. The human sex act had symbolization as a predation by man on woman, his game. In the hunt, the human male left the powerful home base in the female or "game" sphere of the family village and journeyed out into the "hunter" sphere of the wilderness.

Esoteric rites, of which we are all but ignorant, were conducted in the sweat house on the evening prior to departure for the hunt. In the course of these rites, which were led by the Chanter who was to lead the hunting party, each hunter in the party was ritually transformed into an animal predator (Luckert 1975). There then followed, in W. W. Hill's (1938a, 88) words, a "complete reversal of the psychology" of the hunters. Speaking of death, blood, and killing ceased to be taboo, as did use of hunting songs. Dreams of death, blood, and killing ceased to be ill omens and instead became good ones. The hunters emulated predators: walking, running, and even sleeping in canine or feline crouch; communicating in animals' growls; referring to each other not as men but as "wolves" or as "predators"; meditating constantly on killing and death; and suppressing natural humor and levity to maintain an attitude of ferocity (Hill 1938a). Claus Chee Sonny, a Navajo Chanter, explained: "The hunters feel very lightfooted; they become fast runners. Their eyes become very sharp in spotting deer.... There is always a 'spirit of knowing' concerning the whereabouts of deer — received either through positive thinking or while dreaming about deer during the night" (Luckert 1975, 63).

At the end of the hunt, the hunters once more engaged in secret rites in the sweat house, apparently to reverse the effects of the rites of commencement. Everything pertinent to the hunt was put out of mind and normalcy was reattained. Only then might a man return to his wife and family. (Hill 1938a; Luckert 1978)

Navajo hunters related tribal variants of the game theft myth as the origin myth of the ritual hunt. The Black God, Crow, hid all the game animals in Black God Mountain, causing starvation for all the hunter species. A Navajo transformed into a series of birds to discover the whereabouts of the game. He transformed into a puppy to be adopted by the Black God's children and taken into the mountain. Once among the stolen animals, he facilitated their escape into the world. Luckert (1975) commented that the hunter's transformations into birds and a puppy alluded secretly to the esoteric shape-shifting rites of the hunt. Every ritual hunt enacted the myth of stealing animals from the gods who control them. The enactments constituted mystical participations in the living reality of the numinous powers that the myth celebrated: predatory maleness and preyed-upon femaleness.

The routine attribution of religious symbol-formation to neurosis in classical psychoanalysis would pathologize the practice of ritual shape-shifting into a predatory animal during the hunt. Ego psychological method pays attention, however, not only to the symbols but also to the functions that they serve. Symbolism is not limited to pathology; it can also be adaptive. Navajo hunting ritualism segregated the hunt as a thing apart from normal familial life. The ritual sphere included further symptoms of guilt over killing. A host of taboos were conservationist of the game (Hill 1938a; Luckert 1975, 1978). The hunt was an esoteric affair, ostensibly because exposure to it was dangerous for women and children (Luckert 1975), but implicitly because of its unconsciously perceived shamefulness and guilt. Moreover, the Navajo have a profound dread of the ghosts of both animals and men (Wyman, Hill, and Osanai 1942) and symbols borrowed from hunting ritualism have a prominent role in witchcraft (Morgan 1936; Kluckhohn 1944). Implicitly, there was a conscious valuation of the hunt as necessary, and an emotional sense that killing was evil and an occasion for guilt.

Conflict of this order might readily generate neurosis. The ritual hunt isolated the basic cultural ambivalence toward killing and raised the conflict to a religious level that both permitted and defined the hunt as an evil domain of predation. The release of instinctual aggression, forbidden in the familial sphere but necessary to successful hunting, became permissible in the hunt through the suspension of normal morality and the establishment of a "hunt superego" in the image of the predator god. This reliance on a surrogate moral authority (Fenichel 1945) was not possible, however, without a sense of guilt for the abdication of personal moral responsibility. The two guilts, the one toward killing and the other for suppressing the first, were then displaced through the hunter's ritual action as a predator. The hunter felt no conscious guilt as long as he manifested it in the socially encouraged form of aggression against game animals. Hunting created guilt feelings, but religious rituals addressed the guilt (Freud 1907; Reik 1946; Ostow and Scharfstein 1954) by transforming the work of hunting into a kind of play. Serving the function of psychological defense, the rituals prevented the formation of individual neuroses that might have arisen had the guilt instead been allowed to accumulate without relief. Navajo hunting ritualism was apparently psychohygienic in function, not despite, but in fact because of the pathological character of its symbolism.

Because ritual hunting is no longer practiced by Navajos, we cannot undertake psychological assessments of individual hunters. We cannot know the attitudes that individual Navajos once had toward their hunting rites. Did they rely on hunting rituals mostly in obsessive manners consistent with defense, or mostly in playful manners consistent with wholesome adaptations? We similarly cannot know whether the coital significance of hunting, of which Navajos were conscious, generally had the unconscious meaning of fixated Oedipal conflicts, or were instead manifestations of mature genitality. Like the uniforms and regulations that govern soldiers, police, and firefighters in Western culture, the rites of Navajo hunters could be used by both wholesome and morbid personalities.

The Coyote Transformation Myth

The diagnostic neutrality of hunting ritualism is indicated, among other manners, by the Navajo's recognition of a pathological condition that they termed Coyote sickness and treated with Coyoteway healing ceremonials. The need for healing apparently arose when the ordinarily psychohygienic function of hunter ritualism failed and emotional disorders became acute.

The Navajo theory of Coyote illness and its cure were set forward in the origin myth of the Coyoteway rite. Three origin myths for Coyoteway are extant (Luckert 1979) but displacement of the original version of the myth seems to have occurred. In Navajo mythology there are two concepts of Coyote (Wyman 1975). Coyote is today primarily the companion of the agricultural god, First Man. However, in an older conception that is still remembered in occasional myths and folktales, Coyote was a trickster god. The extant Coyoteway myths largely pertain to the agricultural figure; but the extinct ceremonial Excessway, which the Navajo classify as part of Coyoteway (Wyman and Kluckhohn 1938), had as part of its origin myth a passage that pertains to Coyote as trickster. This passage, known academically as the Coyote transformation myth, closely resembles the symbolism of the Coyote-way ceremonial and similarly reflects the mythos of the ritual hunt.

The Coyote transformation myth runs as follows. A successful antelope hunter sang both Gameway and Excessway chants as he hunted. In one of the latter he named himself, among other things, as Jimson-Weed Young Man. One day he was employing a Stalkingway ritual of hunting, camouflaging himself as an antelope, when Changing Coyote crept up on him unnoticed. Changing Coyote took off his coyote skin and blew it onto the hunter. The hunter's clothes fell off him, and in these Changing Coyote dressed. Masquerading as the hunter, Changing Coyote went to the hunter's home, successfully deceived the hunter's two wives as to his identity, and spent the whole night going from the one to the other. Come morning, one wife suspected that he was not her husband. The other remained deceived. Appearing as the hunter, Changing Coyote went out to hunt. Although he often pointed his bow, he failed to loose his arrow and so killed no game. Thus several days passed.

Meantime, the hunter who wore Changing Coyote's skin was dying of hunger. He crept under a cedar, ate its berries, and there slept the night. On successive days, he subsisted on a wild cherry bush, Gray Willow catkins, and the fruit of wild roses. The extant text of the myth does not state, but its plot presupposes, that the suspicious wife asked people to search for her missing husband. The myth simply continues with people noticing that this Coyote was not acting as Changing Coyote behaves. They wondered what had happened. When they asked him if he was the hunter for whom they were searching, he could reply only with a coyote bark. Deciding nonetheless that this Coyote was indeed the missing hunter, they took him home, made hoops of wood, and passed him through the hoops to tear away the Coyote skin. The hunter thereby regained human form. The hunter took the skin, crept up on Changing Coyote, and struck him with it. At once the skin stuck to Changing Coyote, returning him to his own form. After these incidents, the hunter received various items of ritual instruction from different Holy People, teaching him to do cures of like kind in the future (Haile 1978).

Treating the shape-shifting of the ritual hunt as cultural normalcy, we may appreciate the cultural perception of abnormality that was symbolized in the Coyote transformation myth. A successful hunter found himself uncontrollably possessed by a coyote skin. His wives found not a man but a sexually overactive Coyote in their beds. In the hunt, he was impotent to discharge an arrow from his bow. The hunter was discovered in this lamentable condition, and he was cured. The possessing agency was not destroyed but returned to the trickster god to whom it belonged.

Implicitly, we have here a hunter, ritually transformed into a coyote during hunting rites, who had found himself unable upon his return from the hunt to end the transformation. In Navajo idiom, he was still "out there" in the predator sphere of the hunt. He had not been "brought to the hogan" of the game sphere of the family life (Luckert 1978, 48).

A notable motif here is the hunter's initial song referring to himself as Jimson-Weed Young Man. In Navajo hunter myth, consumption of potent hallucinogens contained in jimson weed (*Datura inoxia*), loco-weed, and other plants accounts for both the paranoid timidity of game animals and the paranoid murderousness of predators. The carnivores absorbed the toxins through eating the flesh of game in a primordial era. Among the mythic effects of the narcotics was sexual wantonness, which accounted for animal violations of incest and adultery taboos (Luckert 1978). The Navajo did nonetheless employ jimson weed ritually to divine the whereabouts of stolen or lost property (Hill 1938b). Significantly, the origin myth of the Navajo ritual hunt styled every hunter's every act of hunting as a recovery of stolen game (Luckert 1975). Jimson weed is also known to be used to relieve pain in Lifeway ceremonials, but not apparently in Holyway rites such as Coyoteway (Kaplan and Johnson 1964). On the other hand, the sweat lodge where Claus Chee Sonny conducted his esoteric hunting rites was built beside a stand of jimson weed (Luckert 1978). Whether hallucinogens were customarily employed in the esoteric sweat lodge rites of which we are largely ignorant, we may conclude that the Coyote transformation myth describes one Navajo hunter who did become Jimson-Weed Young Man during a ritual hunt. Drug-induced priapism may account for his sexual hyperactivity, and the inability to orgasm that sometimes attends priapism may be reflected in Changing Coyote's inability to loose an arrow from his pointed bow.

On the religio-mythic level, the Coyote transformation myth pertained to a condition of possession by Coyote that was induced through jimson weed and occasioned nervous disorders of various sorts. The condition was resolved through exorcism. The myth discusses a culturally congenial therapy of conditions associated with jimson weed, but the myth should be interpreted more broadly. Because a myth is a tale about a god's powers, it always serves as the exemplary or paradigmatic instance of a larger range of applications than are explicitly mentioned in the story. Jimson weed intoxication exemplified, but by no means exhausted, the range of conditions that were classified as Coyote sickness.

Coyote transformation may more generally be said to have occurred to a hunter for whom the psychohygienic function of hunter ritualism had failed. For him the hunt had become so very abhorrent that he could no longer bear his guilt over being a hunter. As a result, he fled mentally from normal familial life, and the moral responsibility that it entailed, into the domain of predation where he ceased to bear responsibility for his actions, given that he was now possessed by Coyote. He could not now employ ordinary religious rituals to end his shape-shifting because he was no longer acting religiously. Rather, his unconscious was employing symbols of religious origin to generate culturally abnormal neurotic behavior.

As it was portrayed in the Coyote transformation myth, Coyote sickness was an ethnopsychiatric example of posttraumatic stress disorder (formerly, traumatic neurosis; Fenichel 1945). Whether a single traumatic event or the strain of protracted stress exhausted the ego's defenses, the hunt became traumatic. The religious fantasy of playing an animal predator lost its quality as fantasy and instead became compulsive. The fantasy had allowed the hunter to suppress his guilt feelings, to attribute responsibility to the "hunt superego" of Coyote, and finally to displace his guilt through hunting ritualism. Trauma instead forced the burden of guilt directly onto the hunter. Coyote, who alone was responsible for guilt in hunting, was consequently forced onto the hunter as the hunter's own identity. A reaction-formation was instituted as well. Once identified with Coyote, the hunter became excessively aggressive in defense against the moral implications of familial values, which he could no longer tolerate consciously and instead subjected to automatic repression.

Various classic symptoms of posttraumatic stress disorder can be recognized in the Navajo description of Coyote transformation. The repetition of the traumatic event in the form of fantasies, thoughts, and feelings was symbolized in the myth by Changing Coyote in the hunter's form. The hunter, ostensibly returned from the hunt, psychologically was still reliving the hunt. Sleeplessness or, at best, troubled sleep, caused by preoccupation with the trauma, was indicated in the disguised Coyote's implicit inability to sleep during his night-long sexual activities. His inability when hunting the next day to discharge an arrow from his bow bears interpretation in the Navajo context, where every act of coitus was a predation by man on woman, his game animal. The motif symbolized sexual impotence, an additional symptom of posttraumatic stress disorder. The misery of the hunter, who was unable to put off the Coyote skin, also involved a hunger so severe as to present a danger of starvation despite the passage of mere hours. Reliance on an "oral-receptive way of mastering the outer world" (Fenichel 1945, 125) seems indicated.

Not mentioned in the myth but openly addressed in the Coyoteway ceremonial was the additional expectable symptom of spells of uncontrollable rage. The rage might be expected to have been directed principally against Coyote for reason of his failure to protect the hunter from trauma. The impiety of such anger may account for its suppression in the myth. Changing Coyote was characterized as a trickster but not as evil. The suppression of the anger presumably involved its displacement in the form of anxiety and guilt, additional expectable symptoms of posttraumatic stress disorder. The transformed hunter was anxious about his condition in a depressively forlorn, miserable manner. To the initial guilt over killing, that he continued to feel but could no longer displace successfully, were additional guilt feelings over the breach of taboo that had earned Coyote sickness as its consequence, and over the impiety of rage felt against Coyote. These several layers of guilt, conscious or unconscious, worked to heighten the specifically religio-moral character of the posttraumatic stress disorder.

Coyote transformation differed from a Western textbook description of posttraumatic stress disorder in one important respect. The reliving of the trauma took the form of ritual behavior as well as of fantasies, thoughts, and feelings. The posttraumatic stress disorder presupposed the psychohygienic religious ritualism, whose defensive function continued to operate with diminished effectiveness. The onset of the neurosis commenced, as it were, at a stage of partial defense. The religious ritual provided both some cognitive distance from the full impact of the trauma and a behavioral mode for belated mastery (Fenichel 1945).

Coyoteway

With an understanding of the psychological implications of its cultural context, we may now examine the Coyoteway ceremonial itself. In 1974, Luckert recorded a nine-night ceremonial of Coyoteway, a Holyway that had previously been regarded as having been extinct as early as 1910. As with all other nine-night Navajo ceremonials, Coyoteway was esoteric, was held in a sweat lodge consecrated for the purpose, and consisted of a four-night "misfortune part," a four-night "blessing part," and a summation or conclusion on the ninth night for which the Navajo have no particular term.

The major thrust of the misfortune part consisted of a ritual sweat bath on each of the first four days. Various plant substances were compounded into a medicine called *iilkooh*. The Chanter rubbed some onto the patient's skin. The remainder was brewed into a tea that was drunk by all persons attending the rite. Although called emetics, neither *iilkooh* nor the corresponding medicines in other Navajo rites produce vomiting (Luckert 1979; Richard 1970). Luckert (1979) reported having a mystical experience during the ceremonial, but he said nothing of the medicine having been hallucinogenic. An additional medicine, named *ketloh*, was sprinkled on the patient. Both medicines were termed Coyote's water. The ritually consecrated fire produced heat and smoke that filled the sweat lodge. Over the seated patient the Chanter sang chants verbatim from memory. Most described mythic actions by Coyote. All were given in fixed traditional sequences. The chants functionally provided a text for the patient to contemplate during his sweat bath each day, guiding him step by step to imagine Coyote enacting his mythic behavior.

On the fourth day, as the climax of the misfortune part, the chants abruptly changed character. Each chant contained some twenty to forty lines, each of which either commenced or concluded with a refrain. The progression of the chants on the fourth day moved from the third person refrains, "Now he is moving" and "Now he is walking," to the first person "It is I walking!" and "It is I made strong" (Luckert 1979, 94). Luckert (1979, 123) observed that the patient "experienced the presence of Coyote mystically, after the manner of shamanic possession by some greater-than-human divine being." The misfortune part apparently induced an ecstatic identification by the patient with Coyote. Various subsidiary ceremonies and rites were performed. Unraveling of medicine bundles, fire consecrations, washing rites, and other ceremonies aimed by means either of their symbolism or their ritual awesomeness to reinforce the ecstatic transformation of the patient into Coyote. The term misfortune part presumably referred to the deliberate, ecstatic induction of the very complaint that the patient suffered.

The second four nights and days of Coyoteway comprised the blessing part. Basket-drum ceremonies were held in the evenings and sandpainting ceremonies in the mornings. The basket-drum ceremonies consisted of chants accompanied by a rattle and by drumming on an inverted ceremonial basket. The sandpainting rites consisted of the patient seated on a sandpainting that is erased during the course of the rite. In addition, dancers who were dressed and masked to impersonate deities performed mimes during the sandpainting rites.

On each of the fifth through seventh mornings, a dancer who represented Coyote in mask and kilt entered the lodge. He administered two medicines to the patient, alternately touched cedar twigs to figures in the sandpainting and to body parts of the patient, moved about the lodge, and howled in taking ownership of the consecrated place. Next he howled at close range into the patient's ears and left the lodge. Luckert (1979, 149) noted that "for some hours after this ceremony the patient remains silent. He seems visibly shaken."

On the eighth morning, the Coyote dancer was a different man, who carried in his arm a stuffed blue fox, symbolic of Coyote. With him were male dancers impersonating Talking-God and Female-God. The masks of Blue Coyote Carrier and Female-God were identical. The patient greeted their approach outside the lodge to receive their blessing. Talking-God danced near, gave his call, and sprinkled pollen on the one sung over. Coyote Carrier approached, raised the stuffed blue fox, and gave his howl. Both dancers next repeated the same actions toward Female-God, treating her as they had the patient. This whole process was repeated from each cardinal direction. Once inside the lodge, Coyote Carrier lay the stuffed fox on a blanket, its function having been completed. Talking-God sprinkled pollen, cornmeal, and medicine on the figures of the sandpainting; and Coyote Carrier administered the medicines as in the previous days' mimes (Luckert 1979).

To summarize, the first mimes had Coyote take possession of the sweat lodge and possess the patient. In the final mime, Coyote was exteriorized as the "coyote skin" of the stuffed fox. In Navajo religious anthropology, all supernaturals, personified natural phenomena, plants, and animals have an inner form that is anthropomorphic. In Berard Haile's (1943) view, the inner form is the indestructible life essence, whereas the physical form is a cover or attire, rather than a necessary place of residence. Hence, for example, the sun, meaning the solar orb, has as its inner form the day carrier, the anthropomorphic supernatural who carries the sun disk. In a similar fashion, Blue Coyote Carrier would signify the true life essence of the god. His coyote-skin coat is no more than the animal form that he animates or carries. Because the patient is possessed by the coat rather than by Blue Coyote Carrier, the patient's reconciliation with the god, who had himself exteriorized his coat, had as its necessary implication the symbolic exorcism of the patient's state of possession.

In the three-dancer mime, Talking-God's presence presupposed his role in the tribal initiation ceremonial of Nightway, with its night vigil symbolic of death and rebirth (Matthews 1902; Sandner 1979). Female-God, if she is to be identified with the goddess called White Shell Woman and Changing Woman, would invoke the parallel motifs in the girl's puberty initiation, the Kinaalda (Frisbie 1967). Whatever her identity, Female-God alluded to the domain of familial life. Although present and blessed by the two masculine deities, she herself remained inactive and identifiable with the patient, who was now himself entering the domain of familial life.

Like the idea of sandpainting, the designs of the Coyoteway sandpaintings and the chants sung over them were of agricultural and Pueblo inspiration. Reference was made in these chants to the different concept of Coyote that occurs in agricultural myths, where he figures as a companion to First Man. The assimilation of agricultural sandpainting ceremonies to the older, shamanic ceremonial nonetheless displayed psychological consistency, not in the minutiae of the sandpaintings' symbolism, but in their general structure as rites. Each morning, a sandpainting was completed by the Chanter and his assistants before the patient first entered the lodge. Once the patient sat on the sandpainting, cedar twigs were touched alternately to its figures and to the patient's body, guiding meditations by accomplishing a series of identifications. Lastly, the patient went outside and the sandpainting was erased (Luckert 1979). The Navajo explained the removal of the sandpainting as a removal of the illness. Once again, a symbolism of exorcism can be recognized.

The chants sung in the basket drum ceremony each evening followed their own progression. The climactic series of chants on the eighth evening had the following sequence of refrains:

> With my Mind I walk …
> I am looking for my Mind …
> I have found my Mind …
> I am bringing back my Mind …
> I am reviving my Mind …
> Now my Mind is walking with me …
> Now my Mind is remade for me …
> Now my Mind returns with me …
> Now I am sitting with my Mind …

... everything is made Happiness.
... they are singing for me.
... it is raining for me.
... the blessing is given. (Luckert 1979, 112–17)

Each of these refrains was repeated forty or so times, functionally providing a text that guided the patient through meditations. The chants assumed that the patient was possessed by Coyote and they guided the patient to imagine himself seeking, finding, and reabsorbing his own identity. The return of the patient's identity on the eighth evening accounted for the already-completed exteriorization of the blue fox at the commencement of the three-dancer mime the next morning.

The summation ceremony of the ninth night involved basket-drum chanting and a ceremony in which yucca leaves were burnt to ashes and suspended in water that the patient was given to drink (Luckert 1979). The symbolism associated yucca with the consecrated fires of the sweat baths of the misfortune part. The symbolism probably alluded to the cactus's association with Talking-God (Sapir and Hoijer 1942), who functioned as an exorcist in the final mime of the blessing part.

The misfortune part of Coyoteway reinduced both ritual and ecstatic transformation of the patient into Coyote. The blessing part then reversed these effects. Coyoteway implicitly presupposed that ordinary sweat lodge rites on the hunter's return from the hunt had failed because error had been made in the initial rites at the hunt's beginning. Ritual control of ecstatic possession had therefore to be recommenced at its beginning, when control had first been lost. The reconciliation with Coyote that Coyoteway accomplished involves no more than a re-education, a rite of renewed initiation, into the proper ritual devotion that Coyote required.

From a psychoanalytic point of view, the patient was guided by means of symbolic rituals, sweat baths, continence, various dietary abstinences, perhaps psychoactive medicines, and meditations on chants to experience religious ecstasy of extremely detailed content. There was shrewd heterosuggestive manipulation by which the Chanter aided the one sung over to attain specific insights. The misfortune part provided the insight that Coyote transformation was ritually and hence artificially induced, whereas the blessing part showed it to be entirely temporary in significance. Simultaneous to these insights into the origin of the affliction, the exorcism of Coyote through the chants of the blessing part provided symbolism for displacing the neurosis-causing guilt, by directing the aggression outward at Coyote. The symbolism asserted that Coyote, and not the patient, was responsible for killing. The patient then forgave himself a guilt that was not properly his.

In the final three-dancer mime, the patient was taken the necessary step farther. His aggression against Coyote was an impiety that had been encouraged temporarily to relieve the symptoms of Coyote transformation. The underlying conflict of aggression and piety in the patient's attitude to Coyote was now addressed with a crucial interpretation. Coyote was revealed as a composite figure, consisting of the coyote-skin coat (ritually, the stuffed blue fox) and Blue Coyote Carrier. Aggression toward the coat was not impiety toward the god. Because Coyote was a "transferential figure" (Arlow in Grossman 1993, 760), this feature of the rite constituted an interpretation of the transference, in the technical sense of the term. The presence of Talking-God and Female-God during the mime served to integrate the insights into the patient's general consciousness of moral responsibility in the familial sphere of activity. Meditations during and after the ceremonial provide a format for working through the various insights.

CONCLUSION

The ritual hunt, the Coyoteway ceremonial, and the Coyote transformation myth of Excessway, a part of Coyoteway, are all either extinct or on the verge of extinction. Navajo hunting ritualism was sensitive to the emotional and moral conflicts that hunters faced. Distaste for the bloodshed of the kill, fears for danger during the hunt, and moral concerns for the propriety of the slaughter of game were commonly resolved through the symbolic projection of a god of the hunt — technically, an "animal guardian" rather than a "master of animals" (Paulson 1964). Because Coyote was an exemplary predator, *imitateo dei* provided the basis for a series of ritual beliefs and behaviors whose moral validity had supernatural sanction. The extensive religious fantasies surrounding the hunt gave it a cathartic function, nearer that of play than work. Catharsis through fantasy made the ritual or symbolic actions of the hunt a psychohygienic defense against the inevitable emotional stresses of stalking, ambushing, and slaying.

The defensive and adaptive character of the myth and ritual of the Navajo hunt is established by the myth and healing ceremonial surrounding Coyote sickness. The Navajo distinguished between a myth and rite that they considered normative, and a myth and rite that were devoted to abnormal deviations from the norm.

Coyote transformation, the exemplar of Coyote illness, might be termed a hunting neurosis. Whether gradually or suddenly, the trauma of hunting stripped the symbolic actions of the ritual hunt of their quality as fantasy. Mastery of the stress proved unattainable. The religious ritualism became fixated and its symbolic actions were repeated in emphatic but futile attempts to achieve mastery. Neurotic affectivity and compulsiveness transformed the religious ritualism into a neurotic ritualism, as labile pathological symptoms replaced stable defensive ones.

The Coyoteway ceremonial aimed to alleviate the hunting neurosis while leaving the religious ritualism intact. To this end, it brought the patient to recognize his lack of guilt for his condition, and encouraged him to direct his anger at Coyote. Once the patient's aggression had been sufficiently exteriorized to permit an alleviation of the symptoms of Coyote transformation, the transference onto Coyote was interpreted through the disclosure of Coyote's bipartite nature. His coyote-skin coat was retained as the object of the patient's aggression, while Coyote's essence as Blue Coyote Carrier was made the object of the patient's continued religious veneration. These insights permitted the patient to resolve his conflicts toward his god in a manner not wholly different from psychoanalytic play therapy.

Although the myth and ritual of the Coyoteway ceremonial establish the defensive function of the myth and ritual of Navajo religious hunting, they also represent an exception to the general rule. The hunting myth and rites conformed to ego psychological expectations, but the healing myth and ceremonial is not adequately described as a defense. Writing of Navajo healing, Oskar Pfister (1932) insisted that "there can be no doubt that a cure takes place" (p. 250). He cautioned, however, that "we have no means of knowing to what extent the dissolution of the conflict really and permanently takes place in the unconscious and how often relapses into neurotic tension, or even into the former symptoms, occur" (p. 253). Whatever permanence we ascribe to Navajo religious healing, we must acknowledge that its myth involves more than either symptoms or defenses. The ego psychological approach advanced the discussion of myth, but stopped well short of doing it justice.

5

MYTH AS METAPHOR

Neither the classical nor the ego psychological approaches to myth satisfactorily addressed the religious dimension of myth. Neither psychoanalytic methodology makes a distinction among the genres of myth, legend, and folktale. The legend of Oedipus, an ostensibly historical king of the very real ancient city of Thebes, has repeatedly been discussed as though it were a myth because the classical and ego psychological methodologies have nothing more to say about myths than they have about legends and folktales. For the same reason, the studies that to my mind represent the modal personality approach at its best are two writings by the psychoanalytic folklorist Alan Dundes. Like Boyer, Dundes blends the best of the ego psychological approach with a return to Róheim's emphasis of unconscious psychosexuality. Although Dundes's (1975, 1980, 1987, 1997a) many articles include work on myths, the volumes that I consider his best (Dundes 1984, 1997b) happen to address folktales. The distinctively mythic features of myths are neither necessary to, nor captured by, the classical and ego psychological methodologies.

An unsatisfactory attempt to address the oversight was made by Róheim (1941). Róheim contrasted folktales, which are regarded as fictional, to myths, which are believed to be truthful, by treating them as pre-Oedipal and Oedipal approaches to similar unconscious issues. Folktales involved "wicked parent" imagos that are superego precursors, whereas the characters in myths reflect "the fully fledged superego" with its "different attitude to reality" (p. 278). Róheim's contrast is superficially plausible, until it is appreciated that the same contrast could be made between folktales and legends.

The classical and ego psychological approaches to myth both limited themselves to myths' unconscious meanings and functions. The programs of research were predicated on the assumption that myth-telling cultures believe in stories that are manifestly fantastic, absurd, irrational, and untrue. Few students of mythology today contest Malinowski's (1926, 126) assertion that myths "are what they appear to be on the surface, and not symbols of hidden realities." Most scholars assume that myth-telling cultures believe in the supernatural beings and events of myths in a literal, historical sense (Eliade 1963). Complementary results are obtained when myth is considered not as a genre of folklore but as a type of thought. Theoreticians have repeatedly suggested that mythic thought consists of an uncritical treatment of symbols as realities (Levy-Bruhl 1923, 1926; Arbman 1939; Leenhardt 1979; Cassirer 1959). The attraction to cultural relativism owes in part to an unwanted implication of these views. If myths mean no more than they say, myth-telling cultures must be, at best, credulous and childlike.

Several academic authorities have dissented from the scholarly consensus on myth. They reject literal interpretations of myths and instead regard myths as symbolic expressions of religious ideas whose symbolic character is consciously known and understood by the cultures that tell the tales (Zimmer 1946; Bultmann 1953; Otto 1954; Campbell 1959; Jensen 1963).

A complementary opinion has also been voiced by occasional psychoanalysts. My analysis of the Coyoteway transformation myth as an illustration of religious ideas embodied by the Coyoteway ceremonial uses their approach, but its general principles have broader application than healing myths alone.

SILBERER'S ANAGOGICAL APPROACH

Herbert Silberer (1882 to 1923) was an academic psychologist who joined the Vienna Psychoanalytic Society in 1910. Silberer (1909, 1912) brought with him an experimental technique for inducing hypnagogic hallucinations, the imagery beheld while in the process of falling sleep. As Silberer drifted toward sleep, he deliberately entertained verbal ideas. Next he involuntarily experienced hypnagogic hallucinations. During the hallucinations, he accepted their imagery at face value, as images are during dreams. However, upon alerting from the hypnagogic state, he found the symbolic meaning of the imagery to be self-evident. The same ideas that he had entertained consciously prior to the onset of his hypnagogic state had recurred in symbolic form as the contents of hypnagogic hallucinations. The imagery symbolized thoughts that had been entertained as verbal ideas immediately prior to the images' hallucination. Silberer concluded that autosymbolic symbols depended on the same "considerations of representability" (Freud 1900) that contributed to the dream-work. They were pictorial, could express neither negation nor the conditional, and so forth. However, the autosymbolic symbolism did not involve the additional symbol-forming processes of condensation and displacement. Freud (1914, 97) considered Silberer's discovery of autosymbolic imagery "one of the few indisputably valuable additions to the theory of dreams."

Silberer's discovery of autosymbolic hallucinations led him to a surprisingly modern theory of myths. Silberer rejected the theories of myth that were popular in the late nineteenth century, which interpreted myths as allegories of the sun, moon, stars, weather, and other natural phenomena (Dorson 1955). An allegory is "a narrative in which the agents and action, and sometimes the setting as well, are contrived not only to make sense in themselves, but also to signify a second correlated order of persons, things, concepts or events" (Abrams 1971, 4). However, myth-telling cultures do not provide allegorical interpretations of their myths, and Silberer (1912) inferred that they are unable to express the ideas of their myths in forms other than the images and narratives of myths. "Actually, modern ethnological and linguistic research contends that myths are not metaphoric expressions, allegory-like pictures deliberately invented by primitive people, but rather the only possible expression of their conception of nature, at the time, and for their mental development, adequate" (p. 212).

The next step in Silberer's reasoning was a profound insight. Where the majority opinion concluded that myths are irrational, Silberer thought otherwise. Unlike dreams, autosymbolic hallucinations, and other phenomena that cast ideas into the form of images, myths use imagery to express ideas that have never been expressed as verbal abstractions:

> Let us not forget that there are two avenues open for the exploration of symbols. One of them leads through dreams, neuroses, autosymbolic hallucinations, and the like. To me it seems that in these the symbol appears as a substitute for something that I could under normal conditions clearly grasp, think, or feel: a thought which in daytime — assuming an intact psychic

> apparatus — would be entirely clear, presents itself in my dream, etc., symbolically. Here the symbol appears when I am *no longer in command* of the idea underlying it. If we now consider the developmental history of human knowledge, if we remember how, generation after generation, man pursues knowledge through series of images and mythologies — then the symbol appears as a substitute for ideas of which humanity has *no command as yet*. The conditions favorable to symbol-formation may be reached either by advancing toward or by receding from the idea represented by the symbol. (pp. 216–17)

The differences between these two types of symbol may be found in every culture. In the type of symbol-formation discussed by Freud (1900), symbols express ideas that can be expressed more effectively by existing, linguistically expressed, abstract ideas. Consider an expression belonging to the secret language of Inuit shamans that permitted them to speak with each other in public without being understood by anyone but themselves. Shamans among the Copper Inuit used the word *tulorialik* (the one with fangs) as a euphemism for *nanuq* (polar bear; Rasmussen 1932, 100). The expression presumably referred to the polar bear's habit of hunting people. The shamans could have expressed the concept of a man-eater in so many words. However, they preferred to use the concrete image of fangs as a symbol for the abstraction.

In the other type of symbol-formation, to which Silberer drew attention, the symbols express abstract ideas for which no corresponding linguistic abstractions have yet been attained. For example, the esoteric term *kumaruaq* (the one like a louse), which Inuit shamans used publicly in secret references to *tugto* (caribou), expresses the concept of the imponderably immense number of caribou in the herds that congregated during the migrating season (Rasmussen 1932, 108–9). Because the Inuit traditionally had only a few numbers and could count as high as twenty only by pulling off their boots and enumerating their toes as well as their fingers, they could not express the concept of a prodigious number except through symbolism. In symbols of this type, there is an advance from concrete pattern perceptions into a figurative use of concrete ideas in both thought and speech. The symbols are efforts to adapt inadequate images to serve as symbols for abstract ideas, because appropriate verbal abstractions have not as yet been invented or learned.

Silberer's contentions that there are two types of unconscious symbol-formation won general acceptance among psychoanalysts (Rank and Sachs 1913; Jones 1916; Fenichel 1945). Melanie Klein (1930) added that symbols of the second type have adaptive functions. Through their projection onto external reality, they form the basis of a person's worldview (see also Isaacs 1948; Milner 1952; Rodrigué 1956; H. Segal 1957, 1978).

Silberer appreciated that the type of symbol he was attributing to myths was correctly termed a metaphor. He made the additional point that people may have two points of view about their myths. People may treat mythic imagery as reality; that is, they may reify the metaphors. People may instead know that the symbolism is metaphoric but be unable to articulate the symbolism's meaning in a nonmetaphoric manner. Silberer (1912) wrote:

> A people which speaks in metaphors does not experience what it says as metaphoric; the symbols it uses are regarded by it not as symbols but rather as realities; though a few exceptional individuals, ahead of their times, may know or sense that besides the current conceptions there are others which come nearer to the truth.... Let us recapitulate, no one whose apperception is symbolic can at the time be clearly aware of the fact or of its extent.
>
> To recognize a symbol — or in general, any picturing — as such, presupposes the achievement of a more advanced level of psychological development than that on which the symbol was created. Mythological conceptions had to be outgrown before they could be recognized for what they were. (pp. 212–13)

Although Silberer assumed that there had been a prehistoric phase in cultural evolution when the bulk of the world's myths were developed, he also postulated the continuous origin of mythology: "The mythological does not cease to exist: its creation and subsequent recognition will presumably continue for all time. The state of affairs in the psychology of the individual is analogous. Here, too, a higher vantage-point must be reached before a symbol can be recognized as such" (p. 214).

Silberer's theory of the formal nature of myth had an important corollary. A Freemason (Silberer 1920–21), Silberer was familiar with the persistence in Freemasonry of the traditional view of myth that had been held from late antiquity until the rise of the nature allegory school in the mid-nineteenth century. The traditional view had treated myths as allegorical presentations of moral, metaphysical, and other religious ideas (Seznec 1953; Feldman and Richardson 1972; Lamberton 1986). Silberer regarded myths as metaphoric rather than allegorical, but he otherwise preserved a traditional perspective. In the course of a book on alchemy, Silberer (1914) proposed an anagogic (i.e., a mystical or spiritual) approach to the interpretation of myths. He suggested that alchemical symbols simultaneously had three levels of meaning: the chemical, which interprets alchemical writings as cryptic accounts of chemistry; the anagogic, which is moral and/or mystical; and the psychoanalytic, which pertains to unconscious sexuality. "The chemical content in alchemy is, so to speak, what has been purposely striven for, while the rest came by accident, yet none the less inevitably" (p. 327). Silberer offered the following examples of the psychoanalytic and anagogic meanings of alchemical symbols:

Destroying (castration)	**Introversion**
Mastery	Mastery of oneself
Love of combat	Warring against oneself
Libido	Sublimated libido
Sexual life, incest	Regeneration
Hypercriticism, fussing	Knowledge
Joy in change; improvement	Changing oneself

(Silberer 1914, 267–68)

Silberer suggested that "a more careful inquiry into the mechanism of the psychic powers in the development of mysticism, would show in greater detail how everything that happens is utilized toward introdetermination in the process of education" (p. 264). Alchemists did not deploy obscure symbols in irrational ways. In their manipulations of symbols, they were manipulating the manifest content of psychological phenomena that were well known to psychoanalysis, in manners that were coherent for their development as mystics.

Silberer inferred that parallel circumstances were at work in the shaping of mythology:

> Modern investigation of myths has, in my opinion, sufficiently shown that we are here concerned with a nucleus of natural philosophy (comprehension of astral and even of meteorological processes, etc.) around which legendary and historical material can grow.... the psychoanalytic and the anagogic interpretations are possible alongside the scientific. (pp. 328–29)

Silberer thought it improper for psychoanalysts "to treat as a negligible quantity or to ignore altogether the scientific content (nature nucleus) of the myths" (p. 330). It was not a question of doing either nature mythology or psychoanalysis, but of doing both (p. 331).

In his memoirs, C. G. Jung (1973, 205) stated that he corresponded with Silberer about his book on alchemy at the time of its first publication. Jung did not take up an interest in alchemy until 1928, but he was immediately impressed with Silberer's "anagogic or constructive point of view." Interestingly, Jung soon developed his distinctive system of psychotherapy, which manipulated symbols at their anagogical level much as Silberer claimed alchemists had done (Merkur 1993a, 50–54).

Silberer gained Freud's praise for his theories of hypnagogic hallucinations, myths, and alchemy; but when Silberer claimed that dreams can be interpreted anagogically, he encountered Freud's opposition. Freud (1901a, 69) recognized that "the dream-thoughts ... are not clothed in the prosaic language usually employed by our thought, but are on the contrary represented symbolically by means of similes and metaphors, in images resembling those of poetic speech." In additions to later editions of *The Interpretation of Dreams*, Freud (1900, 562; 1916–17, 237) allowed that some dreams support both psychoanalytic and anagogical levels of interpretation, but he insisted that most do not (Frieden 1990, 32). Personal relations between Silberer and Freud became strained. Although Silberer remained devoted to Freud, Freud rejected him, as he had earlier turned against Adler and Jung. In 1922 Freud wrote Silberer, requesting an end to personal contacts. He also published a detailed criticism of Silberer's views on dreams.

Referring to a particular dream that he had presented, Freud (1922) took exception to Silberer's "superficial" observation of "the expression of an abstract idea, here, as usually, with an ethical reference" (p. 216). Freud asserted that at a "deeper investigation ... reveals ... a chain of phenomena belonging to the region of the repressed life of the instincts" (p. 216). Freud explained that "Silberer who was among the first to issue a warning to us not to lose sight of the nobler side of the human soul, has put forward the view that all or nearly all dreams permit such a two-fold interpretation, a purer, anagogic one beside the ignoble, psychoanalytic one" (p. 216). Freud went on to raise the objection that double meanings of the type cannot be found in dreams, although they do occur among psychoanalysands' associations during treatment. Freud also objected to Silberer's claim that the two lines of interpretation proceeded in parallel:

> The contrast between the two themes that dominate the same series of ideas is not always one between the lofty anagogic and the low psychoanalytic, but one rather between offensive and respectable or indifferent ideas — a fact that easily explains why such a chain of associations with a twofold determination arises. In our present example it is of course not accidental that the anagogic and the psychoanalytic interpretations stood in sharp contrast to each other; both related to the same material, and the later trend was no other than that of the reaction-formations which had been erected against the disowned instinctual impulses. (p. 216)

Here, as previously with Adler and Jung, and later with Rank, what was at stake for Freud was almost certainly his followers' abandonment of his theories of psychosexuality. During the first decade of his psychoanalytic work, Freud had paid a very high personal price in terms of social ostracism, denial of university employment, denial of university facilities, personal vilification and slander, and, of course, anti-Semitism, precisely because he championed an extension of the concept of sexuality. Every time one of his disciples devised a theory that deleted or downplayed the unconscious importance of infantile and adult psychosexuality, Freud broke off relations. Freud was resolutely dedicated to his theory, not only intellectually, but also in charting the direction of the psychoanalytic movement that he founded. He wrote of his work as a third blow to human narcissism, which ranked with the Copernican and Darwinian revolutions; his efforts were rewarded with nothing short of a revolution in the practices of psychotherapy, child-rearing, and education of the young throughout the Western world. It is conventional among Freud-bashers to speak ill of Freud, as though he were too narcissistic to have tolerated competition from his brighter disciples; but he got on extremely well with other brilliant disciples such as Karl Abraham and Sándor Ferenczi. He also enjoyed both intellectual and personal friendships with other extremely intelligent men whose views differed from his own, such as the Lutheran minister and psychoanalyst Oskar Pfister and the existential psychiatrist Ludwig Binswanger. What Freud would not tolerate was squeamishness from a disciple about the theory of sexuality. An explanation of Freud's behavior is perhaps to be found in Abraham Maslow's (1970) observation that ruthlessness is among the behavior traits of self-actualized personalities: the pursuit of a particular excellence often entails a categorical disinterest in wasting time on alternative goals, that other people find severe, harsh, and unsympathetic.

Perhaps because of psychoanalysts' overvaluation of the unconscious contribution to free association, no one seems to have appreciated that as consciously invented narratives, myths necessarily contain materials that dreams, which are unconscious productions, do not. Freud (1900) had argued that the contributions of the day-residue and secondary revision to the formation of dreams provide dreams with a seeming coherence. Why doubt that consciously designed materials in myths impart a full and true coherence at an anagogical level of meaning?

Paul Roazen (1975, 340) remarked that despite Freud's opposition in 1922 to Silberer's formulations, Freud soon revised his own theories to address Silberer's ethical concerns (see also Frieden 1990, 33). In publications the very next year, Freud (1923a, 1923b) introduced his tripartite model of the mind, which attributed ethical concerns to the superego, and he suggested that some dreams manifest superego materials:

> It is possible to distinguish between dreams *from above* and dreams *from below*, provided the distinction is not made too sharply. Dreams from below are those which are provoked by the strength of an unconscious (repressed) wish which has found a means of being represented in some of the day's residues. They may be regarded as inroads of the repressed into waking life. Dreams from above correspond to thoughts or intentions of the day before which have contrived during the night to obtain reinforcement from repressed material that is debarred from the ego. When this is so, analysis as a rule disregards this unconscious ally and succeeds in inserting the latent dream-thoughts into the texture of waking thought. (Freud 1923b, 111)

In *Unconscious Wisdom* (Merkur 2001), I extended the thesis of Thomas M. French and Erika Fromm (1964) that the latent content of every dream is an attempt at problem solving. I attribute the problem solving to the unconscious superego and find, as a datum of clinical experience, that every dream can be interpreted both from above and from below. A similar technical recommendation could also be derived from Brenner's (1982) view of dreams as compromise formations to which the id, ego, and superego all contribute. There is a difference, however, between Silberer's anagogical interpretations and a concern with superego content in dreams. Myths are stories that postulate metaphysical powers. The tales portray paradigmatic metaphysical happenings to illustrate metaphysical principles. The superego's concerns, in contrast, are with human relationships. The superego's database is partly derived from cultural traditions about ethical behavior (Freud 1930); but its thinking processes involve empathy, role playing, moral reasoning, and other forms of interpersonal problem solving that I collectively term relational thinking (Merkur 2001). Conventional ideas about the so-called savage superego conflate the superego with defensive operations (Fairbairn 1963); they attribute unconscious self-punishment to the superego, as though the superego were not responding to the ego's denial of responsibility for on-going wrong-doing (compare Symington 1993) — chiefly, for identifications with the aggressor.

Freud's treatment of Silberer — intellectual disagreement, a rupture in personal relations, and the introduction of a major advance in psychoanalytic theory in implicit but unacknowledged improvement of the rejected innovation — followed the pattern of Freud's breaks with Adler and Jung and preceded the break with Rank. Of the four, Silberer alone did not make an independent reputation after his rejection by Freud. Silberer committed suicide the following year (Roazen 1992, 338–41).

A small portion of Silberer's view of myth entered the psychoanalytic mainstream through an article by Ernest Jones that was for many years the classic psychoanalytic statement on symbolism (Rycroft 1977). Jones (1928) proposed technical terms by which to distinguish the two levels of myth interpretation:

> Let us take for instance the custom of throwing rice at weddings, which used to be general in the days of my youth, but which has now been replaced by the use of confetti. It would doubtless be agreed that the rice in this context represents the idea of fertility, and the act of throwing it the corresponding wish in respect of the bridal couple. Psycho-analysts would say that the rice is an *emblem* of fertility, but a *symbol* of seed. (p. 11)

In choosing the word *emblem*, with its history going back to the European emblem books of the sixteenth and seventeenth centuries, Jones retained Silberer's concept while avoiding the discredited term anagogic.

METAPHOR THEORY

Silberer's suggestion that myths are constructed out of metaphors anticipated the development of modern theories of metaphor by more than a generation. The philosopher Stephen C. Pepper (1935, 1942), whose views were taken up by anthropologists, suggested that root metaphors lie at the basis of world theories:

> The traditional analogical method of generating world theories.... in principle seems to be this: A man desiring to understand the world looks about for a clue to its comprehension. He pitches upon some area of commonsense fact and tries if he cannot understand other areas in terms of this one. This original area becomes then his basic analogy or root metaphor.... a great deal of development and refinement of a set of categories is required if they are to prove adequate for a hypothesis of unlimited scope. Some root metaphors prove more fertile than others, have greater powers of expansion and of adjustment. These survive in comparison with others and generate the relatively adequate world theories. (Pepper 1942, 91–92)

Pepper suggested that both in classical Greece and at present there are "four world hypotheses of about equal adequacy" which he named for their root metaphors: "formism, mechanism, contextualism, and organicism" (pp. 98–99). Because each world hypothesis is determined by its root metaphors (p. 96), each world hypothesis is autonomous (p. 98). It can be evaluated for its adequacy, but cannot reasonably be made the basis for criticizing others (p. 98). In addition, "the cognitive value of a hypothesis is not one jot increased by the cognitive errors of other hypotheses" (p. 101).

Where Pepper argued that the major contemporary philosophies are premised on four basic metaphors, Suzanne K. Langer's (1942) philosophy of symbolism and language discussed metaphors in general. Langer innovated, among other manners, by consciously integrating psychoanalytic ideas in her work as a philosopher. She cited Freud and Rank, but her ideas about metaphors were in agreement with those of Silberer. She recognized metaphors as a means for attaining new ideas:

> In a genuine metaphor, an image of the literal meaning is our symbol for the figurative meaning, the thing that has no name of its own. If we say that a brook is laughing in the sunlight, an idea of laughter intervenes to symbolize the spontaneous, vivid activity of the brook....
>
> Metaphor is our most striking evidence of *abstractive seeing*, of the power of human minds to use presentational symbols.

> Every new experience, or new idea about things, evokes first of all some metaphorical expression. As the idea becomes familiar, this expression "fades" to a new literal use of the once metaphorical predicate, a more general use than it had before. It is in this elementary, presentational mode that our first adventures in conscious abstraction occur.... It is the power whereby language, even with a small vocabulary, manages to embrace a multimillion things. (Langer 1942, 139–41)

Like Silberer, Langer distinguished between the manifest content of metaphors and the understanding that leads to their recognition as such:

> It is characteristic of figurative images that their allegorical status is not recognized. Only a mind which can apprehend *both* a literal and a "poetic" formulation of an idea is in a position to distinguish the figure from its meaning. In spontaneous envisagement there is no such duality of form and content. (p. 149)

Ego psychologists initially regarded metaphors with suspicion. Ella Freeman Sharpe (1937), David Beres (1965), and Benjamin B. Rubinstein (1972) agreed that the choice of metaphors was sometimes determined by unconscious factors, the psychoanalysis of which was warranted. Metaphor theory entered psychoanalysis in the 1950s with the clinical technique termed "interpretation within the metaphor." Rather than to challenge the unreality of a child's symbolic productions, Rudolf Ekstein and Judith Wallerstein (1956) used the same language in a metaphoric manner "in order to convey understanding of his inner world and feelings in the only way immediately available to the patient" (pp. 309–10). Discursive interpretation, which superseded the metaphor, was recommended as a second phase of the technique. "In metaphoric interpretation, in which the therapist's immediate response uses the metaphor of the patient's communication, there follows rapidly an explication which elaborates meaning and intent in mature secondary-process language" (p. 310). Following its introduction as a technique for working with children, "interpretation within the metaphor" became a standard technique in clinical psychoanalysis for patients of all ages (Cain and Maupin 1961; Aleksandrowicz 1962; Caruth and Ekstein 1966; Lindén 1985; Szajnberg 1985–86).

Arlow (1969) initially reasserted the classical technique for working with metaphors. "In metaphor, as in dreams, a single phrase or expression may be the conscious representative of unconscious fantasy activity" (p. 7). The result was a treatment of metaphors that was consistent with Arlow's approach to myths. "The aesthetic effectiveness of metaphor in literature is derived, in large measure, from the ability of metaphorical expression to stimulate the affects associated with widely entertained, communally shared unconscious fantasies" (p. 7). Harold M. Voth (1970) recommended inviting patients to free associate to their metaphors. Norman Reider (1972) likened metaphor to play and dreams, in which unconscious materials have increased access to consciousness. He defined play as "a kind of metaphor in action" (p. 468).

Although contemporary theories of metaphor were introduced by Silberer, Pepper, and Langer, they first achieved popularity in the 1970s, when historians of science began to remark that moments of scientific creativity tend to take form as metaphors or analogies (Hesse 1970; Barbour 1974; Leatherdale 1974; MacCormac 1976). Scientific achievements are often expressed in metaphors before more literal formulations are devised. These findings in the history of science then fed back into the studies of literature, linguistics, and philosophy, where metaphor came to be recognized as an element of thought as well as speech (Lakoff and Johnson 1980, 1999; Lakoff 1987, 1993; Lakoff and Turner 1989; M. Turner 1987).

Following the shift in the scientific reputation of metaphor, psychoanalytic writers began to embrace Langer's understanding that metaphors are efforts to express concepts. They concluded that metaphors are diagnostically neutral (Wright 1976; Rogers 1978; Siegelman 1990). Interpretation within the metaphor did not necessarily have to be followed by a restatement in discursive language. "Those metaphoric interpretations that aim at capturing the client's experience and meaning in the language of the client without going beyond what the client has presented have the greatest potential of being accepted by the client" (Kopp 1995, 121). Melnick (1997) conceptualized oral, anal, and phallic symbolism as a developmental sequence among metaphors. "Many character traits as well as certain conflicts and symptoms are ... the metaphorical — or sometimes metonymic — expressions of early experiences connected with one or another bodily zone" (p. 1011).

Modern metaphor theory also led to a reconceptualization of the task of psychoanalysis. Stanley A. Leavy (1973) recognized that psychoanalytic interpretation converts the patient's symbols into metaphors. "When we interpret, the data of interpretation are found in metaphoric contexts which are both ideational and affective. Images are entertained with feeling. We interpret when we have been able to extend the series of metaphors available to our analysand's consciousness" (p. 326). Revisiting the topic of metaphor, Arlow (1979) embraced the modern approach. "Metaphor can be understood in a more general way as a fundamental aspect of how human thought integrates experience and organizes reality" (p. 368). Arlow acknowledged that most unconscious symbols are metaphors. "Psychoanalysis is essentially a metaphorical enterprise. The patient addresses the analyst metaphorically, the analyst listens and understands in a corresponding manner. Under the influence of neurotic conflict, the patient perceives and experiences the world in a metaphorical way" (pp. 373–74).

In Arlow's view, an analyst's task is to make the patient aware of the metaphorical content of the patient's metaphors:

> The transference in the psychoanalytic situation represents a metaphorical misapprehension of the relationship to the analyst. The patient says, feels, and thinks one thing about a specific person, the analyst, while really meaning another person, an object from childhood. Thus meaning is carried over from one set of situations, from experiences or fantasies of the early years, to another situation, a current therapeutic interaction in which the old significations are meaningless and irrelevant. Transference in the analytic situation is a particularly intense, lived-out metaphor of the patient's neurosis. (p. 382)

A similar perspective was advanced by Antal F. Borbely (1998, 924), who argued "that trauma leads to a degradation of metaphorical processes" and

> interpretation uses the metaphorical process in the analysand as well as in the analyst in order to restore the diminished metaphor capacity.... Interpretations, in principle, aim at kindling growth-promoting metaphors in the analysand by linking emotionally charged, isolated images of past and present to each other. The interpretation helps bringing them into metaphorical alignment. (p. 931)

METAPHOR THEORY AND MYTHS

Let us return these findings on metaphor to the circumstance of myths. Like Silberer, Langer (1942) maintained that myths are constructed of metaphors. Myth "presents, however metaphorically, a world-picture"

(p. 177). Addressing the nature symbolism of myths, Langer generalized that "the eternal regularities of nature.... are the most obvious metaphors to convey the damning concepts of life-functions — birth, growth, decadence, and death" (p. 191). Langer concluded:

> The origin of myth is dynamic, but its purpose is philosophical. It is the primitive phase of metaphysical thought, the first embodiment of *general ideas*. It can do no more than initiate and present them; for it is a non-discursive symbolism, it does not lend itself to analytic and genuinely abstractive techniques. The highest development of which myth is capable is the exhibition of human life and cosmic order that epic poetry reveals. We cannot abstract and manipulate its concepts any further *within the mythical mode*. When this mode is exhausted, natural religion is superseded by a discursive and more literal form of thought, namely philosophy....
>
> Ideas first adumbrated in fantastic form become real intellectual property only when discursive language rises to their expression. That is why myth is the indispensable forerunner to metaphysics; and metaphysics is the literal formulation of basic abstractions, on which our comprehension of sober facts is based. (pp. 201–2)

For Langer, discursive thought, which reasons logically with verbal ideas, was a form of symbolism. It differed from nondiscursive thought, such as the imagery in myths, whose ideas may be linked intuitively, or through narrative, but not ordinarily through logic.

Perhaps because of the ill repute of Silberer's anagogic method, metaphor theory has not been integrated with psychoanalytic work on myths. An independent line of research has nevertheless developed an appropriate technique. After he psychoanalyzed some Western Australian myths and songs, Róheim (1929, 1934, 1974) was surprised to discover that their unconscious contents were identical with the aborigines' conscious understandings of the myths and songs. Both the manifest and the latent content concerned conception through coitus. Róheim was never able to explain the circumstance. Reik (1956, 477) proposed an interpretive technique that he termed archaeological psychoanalysis and described as "the analytic study of prehistoric customs, beliefs, and religions by excavating and interpreting the remains of the emotional and mental life of the past." Reik (1957, 1959, 1960, 1961) employed his method in four Old Testament studies that he regarded as "the most important of all his contributions to psychoanalysis" (Natterson 1966, 251). In parallel with the folklorist Propp's (1984, 118) thesis that "the composition of myths and wondertales coincides with the sequence of events during initiation," Reik interpreted the biblical legends of the creation of Eve, the sacrifice of Isaac, and the Sinai covenant as symbolic narratives that concerned ancient rites of initiation. The studies were unfortunately marred by Reik's use of Tylor's theory of survivals to explain why the analytic method worked. David Bakan (1979), a humanistic psychologist, analyzed the biblical text to understand what he considered to be the conscious and unconscious intentions of the authors. Having studied with Bakan, I applied the method in several studies of Native North American tales. In chapter 4, I argued that the Changing Coyote myth and the Coyoteway ceremonial of the Navajo both symbolize metaphysical concepts of possession and exorcism. In *Powers Which We Do Not Know* (Merkur 1991), I showed that the myths of the Inuit pantheon, which are separate and unrelated as manifest tales, express a coherent and unified metaphysics; I also have applied the interpretive method to Ojibwa myths and legends of the vision quest (Merkur 2002).

Róheim, Reik, and Bakan each developed his approach to religious narratives by adapting the psychoanalytic method of dream interpretation. Where Silberer's anagogic approach assumed that myths had ethical or mystical concerns, Róheim, Reik, and Bakan placed no limitations on the potential interests of myths. Their method, which may be termed metaphoric interpretation, proceeds by treating myths as though they were dreams, and the further contents of myth-telling cultures as though they were dreamers' associations. "Even if we cannot produce associations to the elements in a myth, we can and should use as a substitute for these associations anything we can learn about the mythical, cultural, and historical context of any given mythic element" (Caldwell 1990, 350). Radcliffe-Brown (1939) independently proposed an anthropological version of the same interpretive procedure:

> We may start with a general working hypothesis that when, in a single society, the same symbol is used in different contexts or on different kinds of occasions, there is some common element of meaning, and that by comparing together the various uses of the symbol we may be able to discover what the common element is. This is precisely the method that we adopt in studying an unrecorded spoken language in order to discover the meanings of words and morphemes. (p. 146)

A metaphoric interpretation assumes that myths may employ any of the processes of symbol-formation that the human psyche can produce. Psychological processes govern the making of metaphors, as they govern dream symbols, but metaphors may potentially address any topic of conscious interest.

When is an element in a myth to be considered a symbol? For methodological purposes, the context of a narrative element — better, a representation of a concrete reality — determines whether it has a symbolic function. For example, when the manifest meaning of a representation is logically inconsistent with the manifest content of the balance of a dream, the representation must be treated as a symbol if the logic of the dream is to be disclosed. As Robert Fliess (1973, 17) remarked, "if a sequence of thought contains gaps that can be closed only by reading certain elements in it symbolically, then they are symbols."

Whatever may be the validity of the theory that myths originate as retellings of dreams (Tylor 1960; Róheim 1952; Muensterberger 1964; Stern 1964), myths resemble dreams — and differ, for example, from daydreams — in the manner of their use of symbolism. A dream frequently turns on or culminates in an event that makes no manifest sense and is instead mysterious. If it does no more, the event obtrudes from the otherwise naturalistic character of the narrative and provides the impression that the narrative has an interior logic of its own. Although myths are less quixotic than dreams, they similarly tend to thrust their symbols forward in fashions that attract attention to them.

As an example, consider the Dog Husband myth as it has been recorded among Inupiaq-speaking Inuit. The tale type, which has an international distribution (Thalbitzer 1921, 389–90; Thompson 1929, 347; Koppers 1930; Kretschmar 1938), is known among the Inuit in several variants (Holtved 1966–67). A Chugach variant from South Alaska (Birket-Smith 1953, 152) closely resembles Amerindian variants (Thompson 1929, 347). Elsewhere in Southern Alaska, the migratory tale has been developed into myths of the origin of local Inuit groups (von Wrangell 1970, 12; Lisiansky 1814, 196–97; Pierce 1976, 20–21; Lantis 1938, 132; 1946, 268; Curtis 1930, 79; Burrows 1926, 81). Each variant is highly individual. However, a fairly regular oicotype, or closely related group of versions, as is consistent with a recent and rapid diffusion, is found among Inuit groups belonging to the Inupiaq linguistic division, at Port Clarence near the Bering Strait, and from coastal North Alaska across arctic Canada to East Greenland. The Inupiaq oicotype occurs in two major forms. As entertainment, the tale concerns an anonymous girl who married her dog (Rink 1875, 471; Boas 1888, 637; 1894, 207; 1901, 164–65; 1907, 496; Rink and Boas 1889, 123–27; Murdoch 1889, 594; Nansen 1893, 271–72; L. Turner 1894, 261; Kroeber 1899, 168–69; Rasmussen 1908, 81, 104–5; 1927a, 89–90; 1930, 101; 1931, 121–22; 1932, 240–41; 1939, 132–34; 1942, 115–16; Holm 1912, 270–71; Thalbitzer 1921, 389–97; Jenness 1926, 80–81; Freuchen 1935, 434; 1961, 236–37; Holtved 1951, 23–26; Mowat 1975, 211–12; Malaurie 1982, 98–99, 242).

With slight variations, otherwise identical stories are told as myths (Boas 1901, 163–65, 327–28; Hawkes 1916, 152; Rasmussen 1929, 63–66, 68–69; 1931, 227–28, 380–82). In the mythic variants, the girl is not anonymous. She is identified with the Sea Mother, one of the greatest Inuit deities. In addition, the motif of the marriage to a dog is replaced by an alternative motif. The girl marries a man with a dog-skin amulet who is really a dog in human form. Because symbols do not have universal meanings, it is important for present purposes only that the migratory tale has been integrated by some Inuit groups within the Sea Mother mythology. The Sea Mother variants are myths rather than folktales, and they have acquired meaning from the religious worldview with which they have been integrated.

To summarize the tale type as it is told of the Sea Mother: There was a girl who would have no husband. Her father despaired and said, "Since she will have no husband, she may marry my dog!" A man wearing a dog-skin amulet came and married her. Next morning he proved to have been a dog that had taken human form. She became pregnant. When it was time for her to give birth, her father took her to an island where she was confined in observance of the birth customs. Her husband, now in dog form, guarded her. The girl gave birth to a large litter. Half of her children were human beings, but half were dogs. Because the dog husband was unable to hunt for food, it was in the habit of swimming to the girl's father, who would load it with meat to carry back to the island. One time the father packed stones together with the meat. The burden proved too heavy for the dog, which sank to the sea bottom. Afterward the father took meat by kayak to the island, and fed his daughter and her children. Seeking revenge for the magic words that had cursed her to wed a dog, the daughter encouraged those of her children who were dogs to bring about her father's death. The dogs badly mauled their grandfather before he made good his escape. With no one now to fetch meat, the girl transformed her clothing or boots into boats, and sent her children out into the world to fend for themselves. The dog and human children became the ancestors either of Indians and Whites or, in regions where Indians were unknown to the Inuit, of inland-dwelling spirits and Whites.

The Inuit myth has been studied from a variety of perspectives (Rink 1898; Wardle 1900; Carpenter 1955; Holtved 1966–67; Fisher 1975; Hodgkins 1977). My present concern is with its metaphoric interpretation. Five elements in the myth are manifestly illogical, and the plot of the myth turns on four of them. The girl's father cursed her to marry a dog. After consummating the marriage, the man with a dog-skin amulet took the form of a dog. The girl gave birth to a litter, half of which were dog pups. Finally, the dog children became the ancestors either of Indians or inland-dwelling spirits. Because these elements are both illogical and critical to the plot, they are mysterious as well as symbolic. Only the fifth symbolic element, the transformation of clothing or boots into boats, is taken for granted in the myth; but it alludes, as we shall see below, to the central symbol of another Inuit myth.

The interior logic of the Dog Husband myth implies the explanation of several of its symbolic elements. We do not know at first whether the father's curse has been efficacious. After the consummation of the marriage, the man wearing a dog-skin amulet takes form exclusively as a dog, but we do not know whether he is a man taking canine form or a dog in human form. The possibility that he is a shaman, who employs a dog-skin amulet to transform himself into a dog, is not disproved until the litter is born. The birth of dog children establishes the canine identity of their father. For this reason, it is only after the children are born that the girl's father decides to kill her husband and the girl herself regrets her marriage.

Distinct from the self-explanatory features of the myth are its presuppositions of metaphysical conceptions known elsewhere in Inuit religion. The efficacy of the father's curse presupposes that words have magical force because they are pronounced by the breath-soul and thereby participate in the cosmic breath-soul that is Sila, the Indweller in the Wind (Merkur 1991, 41–71). Sila indwells within every animal's breath-soul, and as such, can fulfill the magic words by sending the girl a dog's breath-soul. Of course, because the breath-soul vivifies a living body, the entire dog arrives. Again, the dog takes human form because breath-souls are anthropomorphic (Merkur 1991, 19–20). Indeed, Sila is unable to fulfill the magic words by controlling a dog's canine form because external form is produced by the free-soul, which is not subject to Sila's power.

The Dog Husband myth employs the symbol of the dog in a context involving the idea of biological paternity. The symbol had the same significance in another Inuit myth. After learning to speak, the first child born by a woman recounted his life in the womb: "There I was as in a small house. Every night when you cohabited, a dog would come in and vomit food for me to make me grow" (Boas 1907, 483). One version of the Dog Husband myth similarly emphasized the repetition of coitus: "They became man and wife. After that the dog used to come every evening. The woman became pregnant" (Rasmussen 1931, 228). These formulations may be referred to the Nunamiut Inuit theory of conception. Conception is not the product of a single act of coitus. Instead, the father "builds up" the womb child with several deposits of semen that collectively "make the baby" (Gubser 1965, 210). In perspective of this theory of conception, the dog may be interpreted as a conscious symbol for the phallus.

The symbolic meaning of the dog establishes that the girl's description as "the one who would have no husband" was more important than the manifest content of the Dog Husband myth indicated. In Inuit religion, the fertility of the sea was popularly attributed to the Sea Mother. The myth implies that her activities depended on the collaboration of a dog; that is, the phallus of a masculine deity.

The historian of religions Jarich G. Oosten (1976, 60) interpreted the red and white stone amulet, which transforms into the dog in a Netsilik variant of the Dog Husband myth, as an allusion to the Inuit moon god. I would add that the Moon Man was the only masculine numen whom the Inuit explicitly described as the owner of a dog. He was also believed to control the tides and, with them, the movements and fertility of marine life (Rasmussen 1931, 403–06).

In the trance experiences of Inuit shamans, the Sea Mother's sea bottom home was guarded by a ferocious animal that shamans were forced to elude before they could approach the Sea Mother. A dog was specified by Inuit groups in the central and eastern Canadian arctic and in West Greenland (Boas 1888, 585, 587–88; 1901, 119–20, 165; 1907, 92–93, 496; Hawkes 1916, 153; Nansen 1893, 251; Rasmussen 1927a, 30–31; 1929, 66, 126; 1931, 227; Rink 1875, 40, 325). Only the Central Canadian groups explicitly said that the dog was the Sea Mother's husband, but Nungak and Arima (1969, 117) rightly question why the Sea Mother was believed to have a dog unless the Dog Husband myth was of reference. Kretschmar (1938) established that the nether-world dog is associated with the moon in North and South America, Siberia, and Europe.

Interestingly, there are notices from the Netsilik and the Iglulik of shamans' encounters with a bearded seal while journeying to visit the Moon Man:

> Across the entrance lay a live bearded seal; he had to step on it in order to get in, and as he did so it shit and no mistake. (Rasmussen 1931, 238)
>
> At the entrance lay a big live bearded seal, which they had to tread on in order to get in. They trod on the bearded seal and entered the passage, and he heard the bearded seal turn round after they had trodden on it. (Rasmussen 1929, 82)

The reversal of the symbolism presupposed male chauvinism. In descending to visit the Sea Mother, shamans found their way barred by the Moon Man's ferocious dog, which they had to evade. When ascending to visit the Moon Man, they simply stomped on the Sea Mother's seal.

Like the Dog Husband myth, the obstacles that shamans encountered during their trances symbolized the idea of a *heiros gamos*, or marriage of the gods, that was responsible for the natural fertility of the sea.

The conscious intention of metaphoricity can be demonstrated through the analysis of a mythic theme, or *mythologem*, that concerns the Earth Mother of the Inuit. In the Netsilik version, from the eastern part of the Northwest Passage, children originally grew "out of the ground just as flowers grow" (Rasmussen 1931, 212). An Iglulik tradition, from northwestern Hudson Bay, states that women did not originally bear children. When they wanted a child, they went out and searched on the ground until they found one (Boas 1901, 309). The children were termed "the children of the earth." Not all people were equally fortunate to find children. Boys were always more difficult to find than girls (Rasmussen 1929, 354). On Baffin Island, the first children were similarly found lying on the earth (Boas 1901, 178). Another tale concerns the first child born of woman. The woman once happened to wear her husband's boots, which were so large that the boot-strings trailed over the ground. One day the soul of an infant that was on the ground crept up the boot-string and into her womb. There it underwent gestation until it was born (Boas 1907, 483). These several Canadian tales commonly express the implicit idea of parthenogenesis, or autonomous maternity.

Although all versions of the Earth Mother tradition employ the motif that children arose out of the earth before women first gave birth, all uses of the motif do not have the same implicit meaning. An East Greenland myth states that people originally lived in the sky and were immortal. A man fell down and mated with the earth, begetting a daughter. The man then took his daughter to wife, and their offspring populated the world (Worster 1925, 95). The East Greenland myth symbolizes the idea of a *heiros gamos*, as distinct from divine parthenogenesis. It also employs a tale type that differs from the Canadian type.

The West Greenland variants are hybrid versions that combine both the Canadian and the East Greenland tale types. In the West Greenland tale, the first man, a giant named Kallak, was formed out of the earth. He mated with a mound of earth that conceived and gave birth to a daughter. He later married the daughter. All mankind descends from the marriage (Rink 1875, 38; Birket-Smith 1924, 440). The variant presents the ideas of both autonomous maternity and bisexual procreation. Their sequence may symbolize a denial of maternity in favor of bisexuality, but the myth might instead be a mechanical production that combined two tale types because they happened to share a motif. In that the storyteller may not have known the implicit meaning of the tale.

However, another variant cannot be explained so simply. It was told by the Polar Inuit, who inhabit Northwestern Greenland a short distance by sea from Baffin Island. Their tale presents a different compromise between the Canadian and the East Greenland tale types. The earth came into existence by falling down from the sky — soil, mountains, and stones. Mankind had origin in the soil. Children formed out of the earth in places where dwarf willows grew. The children were helpless. Their eyes were closed, and they could not even crawl. Willow leaves covered them, and the soil gave them their food. Another myth tells how women did not originally bear children but found them on the earth. A woman fashioned children's clothes and wandered over the soil, where she found little children. She dressed the children and brought them home to her husband. People originally multiplied in this manner. Dogs had a similar origin. A man who wanted dogs went out carrying a dog's harness. He stamped on the ground and called "Hok — hok, hok!" Dogs came out of tiny mounds of earth. They shook themselves because they were full of sand (Rasmussen 1921, 28).

By deriving the Earth Mother from the sky, the Polar version avoided the idea that she had a husband. An unthinking, mechanical compromise of two tale types cannot be alleged. The storyteller recognized the implicit content of the mythic symbols and resolved the ideological conflict between divine parthenogenesis and a *heiros gamos*. The decision in favor of divine parthenogenesis indicates that the storyteller's choice was conscious, knowing, and deliberate. The idea of divine parthenogenesis, the creation of the many from the one, has its unconscious basis in the unitive thinking (Merkur 1999) that manifests itself in mystical moments as an "oceanic feeling" that "the ego includes everything" and later "separates off an external world from itself" (Freud 1930, 68). A unitive mystical experience may have inspired the motif. Alternatively, unconscious memories of early development may have done so. Infants entertain mother-infant merger fantasies (Pine 1981, 1986, 1990; Lichtenberg 1991; Merkur 1999) in the second year of life. The myth reconceptualized the idea of union from an external point of view by imagining how a goddess might experience it.

My argument that myths are symbolic expressions of religious ideas rests principally on the fact that metaphoric interpretations work. Were metaphoric interpretations forced onto myths, rather than derived from them, the interpretations would not fit the myths as readily and precisely as they do. Psychoanalytic criteria inform only my further argument that myth-makers consciously understand and deliberately select the religious ideas symbolized in myths. Some myths exhibit processes of symbol-formation that are inconsistent with unconscious thought but consistent with consciousness.

In principle, metaphoric interpretation is as speculative a method of interpretation as the philological reconstruction of a dead language. No differently than any other method of interpretation, metaphoric interpretation can never be proven correct in a direct, empirical manner. It can be shown to be plausible but never necessary. It insists on finding rational meaning where none need be thought to exist. Its value and justification arise from its practical utility. It makes sense of nonsense. Exploration of its theoretic consequences occupies the remainder of this chapter.

THE IMPLICIT CONTENT OF MYTHS

Most psychoanalysts would describe the goal of metaphoric interpretation as an interpretation of the manifest content of myths. Such a usage would be imprecise. The manifest content *is* manifest. It is explicit and needs no reconstruction. Correctly understood, metaphoric interpretation reconstructs the *implicit* meanings of myths — a level of content that intervenes between the manifest and the latent. Metaphoric interpretation interprets symbols in so far as they are "emblems" (Jones 1928, 11; Fliess 1973, 7).

Because the emblematic meanings of myths are implicit rather than explicit, they may be conscious, but they are not necessarily so. Dundes (1966) emphasized that it is possible to learn to use symbols without being conscious of their meaning:

> Individual members of a culture are not able to consciously articulate all aspects of their culture. Fortunately, people with virtually no conscious idea of the nature of the grammar of their language are able to speak perfectly well and be understood by other members of their culture who likewise have no conscious awareness of the grammatical nature of their language. (Dundes 1971, 117)

Inuit who were not shamans appreciated myths and used their symbols without understanding their implicit, symbolic meanings. In the words of a lay storyteller, myths narrated "incomprehensible happenings, which our thoughts cannot grasp" (Rasmussen 1929, 69). For this very reason, myths engaged religious interest. "If it were but everyday ordinary things, there would be nothing to believe in. How came all the living creatures on earth from the beginning? Can anyone explain that?" (Rasmussen 1929, 69).

Such an approach to mythology should not be imputed, however, to Inuit shamans. The probability that shamans contributed heavily to the formation of Inuit mythology, as they manifestly did to Inuit legendry, is suggested by several facts. Inuit shamans tended to have greater expertise in folklore than did laymen (Balikci 1963, 392). The best informants on Inuit folklore were often shamans or people trained in folklore by shamans (Rasmussen 1908, 308–9; 1927b, 19; 1931, 207; Gillham 1955, 10; Freuchen 1961, 229–30). The term *onipkaktok* (to shamanize) was used of storytelling sessions by the Inuit of North Alaska and the Mackenzie River delta, but of shamanic seances by the more easterly Copper Inuit, who inhabit the western portion of the Northwest Passage (Holtved 1974–75, 22; Jenness 1922, 191). On Baffin Island, a storyteller sat ceremonially on the sleeping platform at the back of the hut, facing the wall, with his hood over his head, and he recited his tales slowly and solemnly (Boas 1888, 572). Baffin Island shamans occupied the identical position and similarly concealed their faces when shamanizing (Boas 1888, 592–93, 604).

Shamans' understandings of folklore can scarcely have been that of laymen. Inuit shamans employed esoteric languages during seances — indeed, whenever conversing with spirits. The languages consisted, for the most part, of metaphoric circumlocutions. Some of the circumlocutions had outlived their common use in the vernacular and were little known archaisms (for references, see Merkur 1992, 13–23). The esoteric languages were not limited to a few items of special vocabulary. They formed complete argots. The anthropologist Robert G. Williamson (1974, 21) stated that "the Eskimo language is capable of a great extent of metaphorical expression — to the extent that the great spiritual intellectuals of the Eskimo society [that is, occasional shamans] were capable of speaking an entire language using metaphors of every part of speech, for religious, ceremonial, poetic, and mediumistic purposes." Svend Frederiksen (1954, 22) noted that circumlocutions were used, not only in shamans' seances but also in their songs. The following lines are from a comic song that was aimed to lampoon a fellow East Greenland shaman (the quotation marks are the ethnologist's):

> Where was it that he tried to learn the angakoq [shaman] art?
> At the "grave" he sought his training as angakoq.
> Why was he wont to repair to the "grave?"
> He who hides himself must do so in the uncanny hiding-place.
> Where (how) should he get his training as angakoq?
> At the "washing-place" he got his angakoq initiation.
> (Thalbitzer 1921, 355)

Only because the shaman chose to inform his audience that he was employing circumlocutions do we know that he did so. The grave and the washing-place were variant euphemisms for the "uncanny hiding-place" of shamanic initiation. The latter was left unexplained. Not only did the exoteric and esoteric senses of the shamans' words differ, but they involved different perspectives. Shamans might report concerning their initiations that they went to old graves, which opened up, allowing them to enter within (Thalbitzer 1921, 467; Rasmussen 1938, 108; 1939, 59). Although shamans encouraged Inuit laity to believe that shamans experienced scientifically impossible events, the shamans esoterically made no such claims. Neither did they claim that what they had experienced only as the contents of visions were real physical experiences. Religious language was demonstrably metaphoric when it referred to "the uncanny hiding-place" as both an old "grave" far inland and a "washing-place" on the sea shore. Even in a vision, a hiding-place could not be both places at once. The metaphors alluded to religious experiences whose contents we have not been told.

The esoteric languages of Inuit shamans ascribed specific meanings to different symbols and constituted a figurative mode of speech. The figurative expressions referred to things that Inuit were also able to discuss in discursive language. Because shamans were conscious of the metaphoric or figurative character of their esoteric languages, it is certain that they possessed sufficient intellectual sophistication to comprehend the implicit contents of myths. On the other hand, there is no evidence to suggest that they ever attempted exegeses of myths, the results of which were consistent with metaphoric interpretations. Inuit storytellers engaged in the "oral literary criticism" (Dundes 1964, 1966) of some myths, but the interpretations were never of a sort that would transform myths into allegories. Moreover, several shamans have divulged their esoteric lore to Western observers, but none ever offered an allegorical interpretation of a myth.

These facts lead to a surprising but unavoidable conclusion. Inuit who comprehended the implicit meanings of myths apparently did so without ever rendering the meanings explicit. The implicit contents of myths were implicit not by happenstance but by necessity.

THE SUBJECT MATTER AND DEFINITION OF MYTH

Deliberately random rummaging about in world folklore has convinced me that if, for the sake of argument, we were to define myths as narratives containing implicit meanings that can be revealed through metaphoric interpretation, we should arrive at approximately the same corpus of tales that folklorists classify as myths on existing criteria. Before attempting to explain why the correlation is intrinsic to the nature of myth, let us examine existing criteria for the definition of myth in perspective of the evidence of metaphoric interpretation.

Myths are variously defined in different scholarly disciplines. Folklorists and anthropologists tend to regard myths as a genre of oral narratives that may be contrasted to legends and folktales (Bascom 1965). Because myths are intrinsically religious, the most sensitive definitions of the genre have been produced by Scandinavian scholars who approach the genre from an interdisciplinary standpoint in folkloristics and the history of religions. Let us consider two proposals. Lauri Honko (1972, 16–18) advocated an inclusive description of myths as verbal narratives that generally concern "decisive, creative events in the beginning of time." Myths function as examples or models, both by embodying a worldview and by serving as practical models of behavior. In the main, their context is to be found in rites that re-actualize the primordial events that they portray. Âke Hultkrantz (1979, 84) considered Honko's criteria unnecessarily cumbersome, however, and offered an exclusive definition of native North American myths. Myths are believed true. They are set at the beginning of time, and their protagonists are supernatural beings.

Both scholars' definitions reflect the consensus that myths mean no more than they say. The definitions may be revised in perspective of the evidence of metaphoric interpretation. By definition, myths are believed true. The question must be raised, however, as to the sense in which myths are believed true. Rodney Needham (1972) ably documented the complexity of the comparative phenomena that are described as *belief* in academic literature. To the extent that ethnographic religions depend on vision quests, shamanism, spirit possession, spirit mediumship, and so forth, they are experienced religions that take belief for granted. I venture to suggest that attitudes toward myths are consistent. Myths are not merely believed true. They are experienced as true, and belief in them proceeds by way of course:

> The Eskimo believed that the emitting of a word evoked an image, which was actual reality. No one could say that an image, once evoked, by being spoken, was not a reality, though a mental one. The language is a complex of mental images, but both the physical objects, and the words used to evoke them — are, in Eskimo thinking, equally real (Williamson 1974, 25).

Joseph Epes Brown (1979, 106) found the same understanding of mythic language obtained among the Plains Indians of North America. Because a spoken word both makes reference to the topic discussed and has magical force in its own right, myths cannot be relayed without being experienced as true. The historicity of mythic events is irrelevant to the experience of myths as truly potent.

Myths are experienced as true because mythic worldviews presuppose an idealist philosophy. "The Platonic-Aristotelean notion ... the notion of 'fixed species' — with all its pseudophilosophical implications about the timeless will and plan of some master mind ... and about fixed laws and realms of essence within or supporting this phantasmagoria of apparent change ... holds a prominent place in all primitive thought" (Campbell 1959–68, 2,292; see also Eliade 1960, 52; 1963, 124–25; Merkur 1991). Just as an idealist experiences language as metaphysical truths, so mythic thinkers experience myths. Given a mythic worldview, belief goes by way of course.

As a criterion for defining myths, the temporal setting of myths in a primordial era is not completely reliable. Narrative is inherently diachronic. Part of a story is always told before the next part. Because a diachronic format is a limitation imposed by the medium of narrative, the temporal sequence of events within a myth, like that within a dream, is often a mere convention — in Freud's (1900) idiom, a "consideration of representability" — that has no necessary bearing on the myth's implicit meaning. Moreover, the assumption that "the myth is thought to express the *absolute truth* because it narrates a sacred history" (Eliade 1960, 23) is a widely shared ethnocentricity that was inspired by Jewish and Christian belief in the historicity of biblical legend. Edwin S. Carpenter's (1956) report of the time concept of the Aivilik band of Iglulik Inuit did not use Western categories as a point of reference:

> They regard the "past" as merely an attribute of the present, as something immanent in all Aivilik being.... History and mythical reality, then, are not the "past" to the Aivilik. They are forever present, participating in all current being, giving meaning to all their activities and to all existence. (pp. 1–2)

Brown (1979, 103–4) found similar views among the Plains Indians of North America, as W. E. H. Stanner (1964) did among the Australian aborigines. The mythic concept of time is consistent not with the classical physics of Newton, but with the modern, mystical physics of Einstein. Reality is synchronic; time is an illusion of apparent diachronicity.

Definitions of myth in terms of decisive, creative events are similarly untenable for Inuit mythology. As Boas observed:

> The most striking feature of Eskimo folk-lore is its thoroughly human character. With the exception of a number of trifling tales and of a small number of longer tales, the events which form the subject of their traditions occur in human society as it exists now. There is no clear concept of a mythical age.... In none of these creation legends is there any inner connection between the whole trend of the story and the incident of creation. It is not clearly stated, and in many of these stories it is not even necessarily implied, that the animals created did not exist before the creation recorded in the story. The animals created are rather individuals than the first of their species.

> The general conditions of life supposed to prevail at the time of the story are the same as the conditions of life at the present time. (Boas 1904, 2, 4–5)

A few tales from Inuit groups in the Central Canadian Arctic acquired both the conception of the trickster Hare (Rasmussen 1931, 208) and the associated idea of a primordial era (Rasmussen 1929, 253–54; 1931, 208–11) from neighboring Algonkian Indian tribes. Boas's generalizations are otherwise valid for Inuit myths from southern Alaska to Eastern Greenland. The protagonists of Inuit myths are almost always ordinary Inuit. In a few cases, they are animals. The tales often recount adventures of prodigious character, but so too do legends of shamans. Creative events proceed on a scale consistent with shamanism. It is only their implicit meanings that disclose their cosmic significance. Inuit myths invariably conclude, however, with the transformation of the mortal protagonist into an immortal god or spirit; even the assumption of cultic dignity is usually mentioned gratuitously, as an afterthought to the tale as a whole. On conventional folkloristic criteria, Inuit myths might bear comparison with European legends of saints rather than European myths but no scholar has ever denied them to be myths. Hultkrantz (1965) did not hesitate to classify the Inuit tales as myths despite their exceptions to his definition of the genre.

Precisely because Inuit myths defy the conventional criteria for defining myths, their case is instructive. Let us attempt to articulate what makes them mythic. They meet two conventional criteria. They are believed — better, experienced as — true, and their *dramatis personae* always include numina, holy or demonic beings, either before or after the full assumption of their final dignities. They also meet an additional criterion. Like myths the world over, the thematic concerns of Inuit myths are the powers and spheres of interest of the numina. The criterion of theme is important. A myth need not have a numen as its protagonist. In some cases (e.g., in culture-hero myths), the protagonist is a foil, and the numina that are the concern of the myths have the roles of antagonists. However, numina are always the central characters of myths' themes, as distinct from the plots.

Metaphoric interpretation discloses an additional criterion for the definition of myths. The religious ideas that are symbolized by myths are invariably abstract in character and metaphysical in concern. Let us consider, for example, a myth of the Caribou Mother that was told by the Iglulik Inuit of Northwestern Hudson Bay:

> At the time when the sea beasts were first made, there were no caribou on the earth; but then an old woman went up inland and made them. Their skins she made from her breeches, so that the lie of the hair followed the same pattern as her breeches. But the caribou was given teeth like other animals; at first it had tusks as well. It was a dangerous beast, and it was not long before a man was killed while hunting. Then the old woman grew frightened, and went up inland again and gathered together the caribou she had made. The tusks she changed into antlers, the teeth in the front of the jaw she knocked out, and when she had done this, she said to them:
>
> "Land beasts such as you must keep away from men, and be shy and easily frightened."
>
> And then she gave them a kick on the forehead, and it was that which made the hollow one can see now in the forehead of all caribou. The animals dashed away, and were very shy thereafter. But then it was found that they were too swift; no man could come up with them, and once more the old woman had to call them all together. This time she changed the fashion of the hair, so that all did not lie the same way. The hair of the belly, under the throat and flanks, was made to lie in different directions, and then the animals were let loose once more. The caribou were still swift runners, but they could not cleave the air as rapidly as before, because the hair stood in the way, and men could not overtake them and kill them when they used certain tricks. Afterwards, the old woman went to live among the caribou: she stayed with them and never returned to the haunts of men, and now she is called, the Mother of the Caribou. (Rasmussen 1929, 67–68)

Additional versions of the myth were recorded on Baffin Island and in Labrador (Boas 1888, 587–88; 1901, 167–68; Hawkes 1916, 160). The variants appended another episode. After her creation of the caribou, the old woman additionally created the first walrus. She proceeded in much the same fashion, except that she used her boots, rather than her breeches, to fashion the walruses' hides. Significantly, taboos surrounding walruses were referred on Baffin Island not to the Sea Mother but to the Caribou Mother (Boas 1888, 584, 637; 1901, 122–23).

To understand the myth, it will be best to start with commentary — oral literary criticism — that the Iglulik storyteller provided. Once when Rasmussen questioned his informant about logical inconsistencies in another myth, she responded with an enlargement on the myth of the Caribou Mother:

> At the time when Takanakapsaluk [the Sea Mother] had fashioned the great and meat-giving beasts of the sea, there was an old woman who thought the land ought also to have special animals of its own. So she went up inland, far, far up country, away from the dwellings of men, and here she began uttering magic words to create a kind of animal which might be useful to mankind. By means of strange words and their magic power she gave life to something, the body of which became a caribou. But this caribou was nothing but flesh and blood and bones. It had no hide, no skin. So she could find no better way out of the difficulty than by taking her old breeches, which were made of caribou skin, and over these she worked magic in such a fashion that the caribou got their skins from those breeches. This is why we say that the lie of the hair on a caribou skin is just like woman's breeches of caribou skin.... As to where the woman who afterward became the mother of all caribou got the caribou skin her breeches were made of — nobody bothered about that (Rasmussen 1929, 69–70).

The commentary directs interpretation of the myth. In Inuit religion, magic words were believed to have power because, being pronounced by the breath, they participate in the Wind Indweller, the collective breath-soul (Merkur 1991, 57–59). In keeping with this belief, we would expect that the caribou's breath-soul was the only portion of the animal that could be created by means of magic words. This conception is present in the myth in symbolic form. Traditional Inuit religion conceived of two types of soul. The breath-soul was always anthropomorphic, whereas the shadow or free-soul was responsible for the individual form and personality of a creature — man for man, bear for bear, caribou for caribou, and so forth (Merkur 1991, 20). These distinctions inform the Caribou Mother myth. The originally skinless condition of the animals symbolized creatures that had breath-souls but, for want of free-souls, lacked external forms and personalities. The Caribou Mother had to perform a separate act of creation to produce free-souls. For this purpose, she employed her clothing. So understood, the apparent paradox that caribou skin clothing pre-existed caribou proves to be a misunderstanding of the myth. The paradox exists only when the motifs are treated at face value, rather than as symbols. The implicit content of the myth is logical. The Caribou Mother's supply of free-soul substance pre-existed her production of the free-souls of individual caribou.

The balance of the myth describes how adjustments in the animals' external forms, that is, their free-souls, resulted in variations in their personalities and abilities. By these means, the Caribou Mother was able, as she chose, both to protect the animals from hunters and to make them available to hunters.

Taken for granted in the myth was an additional consideration. The type of numen that the Inuit termed *inua* (plural, *inue*; meaning owner or indweller) was a strictly conceived metaphysical category that may best be described as an idea, in the Idealist sense of the term. An *inua* indwelled in and imparted characteristic structure to a class of physical phenomena. An indweller was simultaneously a personal being — a thinker as well as a thought. Always anthropopsychic, an indweller was anthropomorphic whenever he or she happened to be visible (Merkur 1991, 34). Because the Caribou Mother was an *inua*, the myth conceived of her as a personified idea. For this reason, she could not draw on her own substance to create free-souls, and the myth had her employ her clothing. The symbolism was polyvalent. The Caribou Mother's clothing was consubstantial with the external forms (both skins and free-souls) of caribou, and her activity as a seamstress symbolized the *inua*'s manner of creation. Just as she was spatially within her clothing, she created free-souls by indwelling in the substance symbolized by her clothing and impressing the idea that she is upon it.

The time frame of the myth was a mere convention of the medium of narrative. The goddess always behaved in a fashion consistent with her portrait in myth. Only because the Caribou Mother determined ongoing processes of generation was she able to enforce the hunting observances that she demanded. She could refuse to create animals' free-souls, preventing them from being born. She could also alter the shape of the living animals' free-souls, causing their behavior to change in manners that made them impossible for Inuit hunters to kill. The myth was neither arbitrary nor unthinking. It was not a "just-so" story. It was a reasoned theological explanation of the living metaphysical forces to which Inuit hunting rites conformed. The myth narrated first acts as illustrations of the goddess's living powers. Primordial acts of generation were prototypes that exemplified all subsequent acts of generation. The metaphysical powers necessary to accomplish a creative act for the first time were powers necessary to the act as such. Every act of generation was an original and autonomous act, identical with the first.

What occurs in a myth is not any action by a numen, but the typical, defining, and characteristic action of a numen. It is precisely because they are paradigmatic that myths function, in Malinowski's (1926, 84) famous formulation, as a "charter" for religious behavior, rites, and institutions. Rasmussen (1931, 362) asserted that, in traditional Inuit culture, "tales and myths form a basis of their whole religion, their beliefs and their view of life.... the tales are always referred to when, in the course of discussions that turn upon spiritual subjects, questions are encountered that cannot be explained." The paradigmatic significance of mythic activities may be implicit, rather than manifest and explicit. In both events, myths portray and explain the living powers of the numina. Because the living powers of the numina are abstractly conceived and metaphysical in character, myths invariably symbolize abstract, metaphysical ideas. Their implicit meanings and religious functions are analogous to the systematic theologies of the literary religions.

Although the mechanical, one-on-one correlation of myths and rites that was proposed by the myth and ritual school is demonstrably mistaken (Kluckhohn 1942), a great deal more mythology is cultic than is commonly supposed. Hultkrantz (1979) argued that most Native American narratives that were conventionally classified as folktales are believed true and should therefore be recognized as "myths of entertainment." I would add that almost all animal characters in myths of entertainment also functioned as minor spirits through amulets, medicine pouches, and so forth. The Inuit Fox Wife myth was relevant to fox amulets; the Inuit Goose Wife myth to goose amulets, and so forth. Additional myths that did not correspond to cultic behavior had cultic function as "units of worldview" (Dundes 1971). They concerned numina that received no cult but were nonetheless encountered in religious experiences. The myths explain something of the powers, personalities, and habits that the numina were conceived to possess.

Because the temporal setting of a myth is irrelevant to its implicit metaphoric meaning, there is no discrepancy between myths, considered as a genre of oral narrative, and mythic thought, considered as a type of psychic activity. In dispensing with the time frame integral to the medium of narrative, mythic thought remains a faithful symbolism of abstract, metaphysical ideas. It also retains its sociological function as a charter for religious behavior, rites, and institutions. For example, the Chugach Inuit, of Southern Alaska, described *Nunam-shua* (the

Indweller in the Earth) as a woman. A bright light surrounded her. She wore a coat that reached to her knees, from which hung living miniatures of all manners of land animals. She also wore fur boots and bracelets (Birket-Smith 1953, 121). The symbolism may be understood by reference to the Chugach conception of the *shugunra* (free-soul), which has the same appearance as a creature's body but is miniature in size (Birket-Smith 1953, 123). The miniature animals that hung from the Earth Mother's coat were animals' free-souls. The Chugach idea of the Earth Mother's coat, from which hung living miniatures of animals, was equivalent to the Canadian Inuit narrative about the Caribou Mother's clothing, from which she fashioned the skins of animals. Both tales symbolized the living powers of the numina to determine success and failure in the hunt, and so to require hunting rites.

MYTHIC CONCEPTIONS AND RELIGIOUS THOUGHT

Our description of myths is now complete. Empirical criteria suffice for purposes of definition. Myths are narratives that are believed true. Their *dramatis personae* include one or more numina and their themes are the numina's powers and spheres of interest. To these defining criteria may be joined observations that emerge through analysis. Myths contain implicit contents that symbolize abstract, metaphysical ideas. Because the ideas are paradigmatic accounts of living numina, myths function as units of worldview. They often have social function also as charters for religious behavior, rites, and institutions.

These several correlations are determined, so I suggest, through the coincidence of an additional factor: the inherent nature of religious thought. In an important but little-known essay contrasting "Mythic and Religious Thought," the historian of religions Ernst Arbman (1939, 27; see also Hultkrantz 1972) suggested that "religious thought" has its basis in a physical event that is "referred to [a] certain fictive will or forces postulated by faith, in which it is conceived as a potentiality." Proceeding from this basis in the subjective experience of the miraculous, Arbman isolated a distinguishing feature of religious thought. "It is obvious that [a] happening that is so understood is in its very origin of an impenetrable, mystic and incomprehensible character. It may be conceived, or, if faith is strong, experienced, but it cannot be imagined or represented in concrete form" (Arbman 1939, 28). The circumstance with myth is otherwise, because myth is "plastic, graphic, descriptive, visual.... This mythical way of conceiving the divinities has its root in anthropomorphism, which furnishes the gods with human qualities and attributes, both internal and external ... [and] is sometimes so pronounced ... that all differences between human and divine seem to be abolished" (p. 29).

Although I do not endorse all of Arbman's remarks, his defense of the religious character of myths remains cogent:

> Where belief is living ... this [mythic] humanizing of the gods and their actions does not imply any real compromising of their divinity. For in living belief the gods are possessed of power, and it is in this, not in their more or less human features, that their real character, their ... divine nature lies. (p. 39)

The apperception of physical events as miracles is by no means a complete account of religious thought. It is instead a minimum account of the necessary or essential nature of religious thought. As John Bowker (1973) observed, there is no particular difficulty in accounting for the origin of religious ideas, nor for belief in them. It is difficult, however, to account for the failure of humanity, in our majority in all our generations, to exercise doubt much less denial of our religious ideas. "There must be sufficient feedback into experience, whether social or individual, for plausibility to be maintained" (p. 84). More than any other variety of religious experience, the apperception of physical events as miracles constitutes the necessary feedback. Even shamans, who experienced ecstasies, based their religious worldviews on their experiences of miracles (Rasmussen 1929, 32).

In comparing mythic with religious thought, Arbman placed weight on the invisible causes of miracles rather than their mythic conceptions. Religious conviction of the objective reality of numina has its basis in religious experiences. Myths are no more than hypotheses toward which faith may be extended. For example, the Inuit approached their religion, as informants repeatedly stated, in what can only be described as an empirical manner. They trusted their religious experiences as self-evident realities, and they believed their traditions to be based on ancestral observations that were, at least in principle, subject to improvement (Birket-Smith 1959, 160). Importantly, Inuit acculturation often proceeded in a fashion consistent with these claims. Epidemics of European diseases, endured often in advance of direct contacts with Westerners, consistently discredited shamans and prepared the way for Christian missionaries and Western doctors.

Because religious experiences take both logical and emotional priority over myths, Arbman's observations lead me to a fundamental consideration. *In all cases of mythic thought that corresponds to living numina of religious thought, mythic conceptions cannot be regarded other than as symbolic expressions of the corresponding ideas of the numina in religious thought.* In so far as myths refer to living numina, the myths are subjectively experienced as symbols of the numina, and are not symbols only in the view of external observers. For this reason, any narrative that has a living numen's power or sphere of interests as its theme will inevitably contain an implicit, symbolic content of abstract, metaphysical concern and paradigmatic significance. A narrative cannot pertain to a living numen in other than an implicitly symbolic fashion.

The differential factor between religious thought and mythic conceptions is not coextensive with myths' use of implicit symbolism. In living tradition, the differential factor is merely a necessary instance that illustrates a general principle. Once the conscious understanding arises that mythic images are symbols, the full capacity of the human psyche for symbol-formation may be brought to bear in myth making, telling, and hearing.

My contention that living religious thought informs the symbolic understanding of myths has various corollaries. Adolf E. Jensen (1963) maintained that, like all other cultural manifestations, myths are devised to express ideas. With the passage of time and the success of the myths as disseminators of the ideas, myths undergo semantic depletion. They persist in oral tradition, but their original meanings are detached from them. In some cases, the original meanings persist in cultic or secular contexts. In other cases, they are forgotten and lost. In either event, the myths continue to apply the ideas that inform them, but their audiences do not know the ideas. Myths may then be given new meanings that are evident as pseudopurposes when compared with the ideas that remain implicit in the myths. I would add that myths are not abandoned once they have lost their meanings but are instead given pseudopurposes, because myths are self-evidently symbolic as long as living religious thought informs them. Pseudopurposes arise through efforts to explain their implicitly symbolic character.

My findings may similarly augment the position of Carl Wilhelm von Sydow (1948), who observed that European peasant traditions of the spirits of the corn and the wild are intended literally but are disbelieved by those who tell them. Because myths that are believed true are comprehended symbolically, there may be an inverse functional relationship between reification and belief in myths. When religious thought ceases to inform the symbolism of myths, myths become reified, belief in them declines, and the stories come to be treated as fictions.

CONCLUDING REFLECTIONS

Silberer and Langer suggested that myths use metaphors to express concepts that myth-telling cultures lack the vocabularies to phrase in discursive language. Silberer assumed that myths use metaphors to convey ethical or mystical teachings, but Róheim, Reik, and Bakan found that the concerns of myths were more diverse. Arbman noted that the people believe in myths because they experience the gods of myths as living numina. Myths use pictorial imagery to discuss invisible powers that are credited with miracles in the lives of the faithful. Religious faith endows myths with metaphoric relevance to the divine powers that are believed to be at work in the world. The difference between the divine actors in myths and the unseen powers of the world guarantees the experience of myths as metaphors.

Metaphoric interpretations reconstruct the religious ideas that myth-makers have designed their tales to express. The results of a metaphoric interpretation are both of historical interest in their own right and necessary phenomenological preludes for secondary orders of analysis — whether psychoanalytic or sociological. Dundes (1966) recommended that folklorists ask native storytellers and their audiences to provide exegeses of their tales. However, exegeses of the largest part of the world's mythology can no longer be obtained in the field. Not only do many myths derive from ancient and vanished cultures, but also the rich allusions of the myths of living cultures have largely been lost as the precontact religions have yielded to the processes of acculturation. Native informants today regard many myths as fictions and do not know the meaning or meanings that the myths had for their forebears. "Oral literary criticism" (Dundes 1964, 1966) of the once-living myths — as distinct from the fictions that the tales have since become — can seldom be obtained in the field. They must instead be reconstructed at the writing-desk. Moreover, even under ideal field conditions, metaphoric interpretation can never be fully replaced by informants' remarks, because it alone is able to articulate myths' implicit and unconscious dimensions.

6

THERAPEUTIC INSIGHTS IN MYTH

The metaphoric nature of myth has diagnostic implications. The classical diagnosis of myth, from Rank through Róheim, treated symbols as unconscious manifestations and myths as symptoms of cultural psychopathologies. Overemphasizing the distinction between symptoms and defenses, ego psychology reassessed myths and persuasively identified them as defenses. Both approaches shared the assumption that myths are irrational products of unconscious thought. Both may be contrasted to Silberer's approach, which maintained that the anagogical content of myths is conscious, metaphoric, and potentially rational.

Silberer's position was initially resisted and soon abandoned. Ninety years later, Rank's pathologizing seems ethnocentric and condescending, and Silberer's generosity of spirit has stood the test of time. Not only has metaphor been an indispensable form of rational thought in the context of scientific discoveries, but clinical psychoanalysis has recognized the therapeutic value of making interpretations within the metaphor. George Victor (1978), N. Gregory Hamilton (1980, 1990), and Laurie Adams (1990) recommended myths as a source of clinical metaphors:

> The characters and narratives of myths, like fairy tales, literature, theater, and films, can be discussed by psychoanalysts in their interventions, as metaphors or allegories of analysands'

> situations. Through the patients' identifications with the myths, insights into the myths can be understood as insights into themselves, by patients who are able to comprehend and work with metaphors. (Adams 1990, 601)

The usefulness of myths in clinical psychoanalysis has implications for the understanding of traditional religious healing.

Oskar Pfister (1873 to 1956) was a Swiss Lutheran pastor, teacher, and psychoanalyst. He was the first person to apply psychoanalytic principles in the field of education, and he was a personal friend of Freud and his family. Along with Eugen Bleuler, Pfister founded the first Swiss Society for Psychoanalysts. He remained with Freud during the break with Jung and the dissolution of the Swiss society in 1914. Pfister started a new Swiss Society for Psychoanalysis in 1919, which remains affiliated with the International Psychoanalytic Association. The society admitted lay analysts, prompting Freud's (1926b) composition on "The Question of Lay Analysis" (Zulliger 1966).

As early as 1932, Pfister recognized during a field trip to the American Southwest that Navajo religious healing is efficacious because symbols are manipulated in ways that convey therapeutic insight. "Not only the detection of the etiological cause, but also the therapeutic elaboration coincided entirely with psychoanalytic principles, though the conflict was not brought to consciousness" (Pfister 1932, 246). Pfister insisted that "there can be no doubt that a cure takes place" (p. 250). As analogs, he cited Gertrud Behn-Eschenburg's use of "figurative language" in the analysis of children (p. 250), and the function of all art "in which the distress, on the one hand, is recognized symbolically and, on the other, is treated and overcome by a symbolic exposition of reality" (p. 251). Pfister suggested that art "in a broad sense may really be called psychotherapy"; it has "immense value and prophylactic and therapeutic significance in mental hygiene" (p. 251).

To account for the therapeutic effectiveness of Navajo healing, Pfister suggested that the meaning of the symbols is coherent to the unconscious superego:

> How can the unconscious, making use of symbols, lay bare the symptoms? Let us remember that every symptom arises from a repressed inner conflict and that it makes use of disguises to spare the unconscious annoyance. In these religious ceremonies the unconscious of the medicine man speaks to the unconscious of his patient and circumvents consciousness. He

> thus avoids resistance which would have been aroused, had consciousness intervened.
>
> The dissolution of that conflict which had been solved in an unsatisfactory manner by the disease symptom is accomplished by this influence of one unconscious on another.... The repressed Super-ego assumes the responsibility of dissolving this conflict, and the motive for retaining the symptom ceases to exist. (p. 251)

Freud (1913) had made a similar observation a decade prior to his introduction of the term "superego": "Psychoanalysis has shown us that everyone possesses in his unconscious mental activity an apparatus which enables him to interpret other people's reactions, that is, to undo the distortions which other people have imposed on the expression of their feelings" (p.159). Pfister made the additional claim that because symbolic analysis does not arouse resistance, a psychoanalysis that conveys its insights through symbolism may be both more effective and more brief than conventional psychoanalysis:

> The inner reconciliation as [a] result of symbolic understanding takes place in a much more effective manner than if a rational explanation were suddenly given, for such hasty explanation would quicken all the insidious resistances connected with rendering the material conscious.... An analysis thus limited to symbolic manifestations has the advantage of great brevity, because all resistances are circumvented or overridden. (pp. 251–52)

Like Silberer's recognition that myths are metaphoric, Pfister's theory of symbolic healing was a contribution to classical psychoanalysis that was of marginal interest in its time and was never cited by later psychoanalysts. Devereux's (1958) fieldwork among the Mohave Indians of California led him to similar observations, but he reacted in the opposite manner. Where Pfister had welcomed the enlargement of classical psychoanalysis, Devereux protected ego psychology's claim to orthodoxy by stressing the nonscientific character of Mohave religious healing:

> There are ... many ... examples of primitive psychiatric ideas which, while essentially correct, are not truly scientific, as for instance:

> (1) The Mohave have an amazing insight into early sibling rivalry, but only for the reason that the adult, who is constantly under pressure to be overly generous, projects his resentment upon the infant who is about to be weaned because its mother is pregnant once more.
>
> (2) The same tribe has a singularly modern-sounding theory of depression, mourning, and funeral suicide, which is, however, formulated in purely eschatological terms, derived from beliefs about seductive ghosts.
>
> (3) The Mohave are able to identify and describe a special form of agitated depression afflicting old husbands deserted by young wives, because marriages of that type have a specific, although atypical, social and psychological function in that tribe.
>
> (4) Mohave shamanistic psychotherapists inquire into the patient's dreams and demand that, in narrating them, the patient should obey the Mohave equivalent of the basic rule of psychoanalysis. However, the shaman is interested in dreams chiefly because they enable him to identify the supernatural agency — or the witch — responsible for the illness.
>
> The point which such examples illustrate is a relatively simple one: The primitive psychiatrist is never more completely the culture-bound empiricist than when he presents himself in the guise of a sophisticated theoretician, or metapsychologist. (Devereux 1958, 364–65)

Devereux did not marvel at the psychiatric sophistication of Mohave shamanism. Neither here nor elsewhere in his extensive writings on Mohave culture did he offer a systematic presentation of Mohave shamans' intellectual achievements. Devereux (1961) considered shamans to be neurotic. He took for granted that their worldviews were irrational and symptomatic. He strangely considered it irreligious that Mohave shamans made use of empirical discoveries that were based on trial and error.

A similar embrace of empiricism may nevertheless also be found in Inuit religion. The Inuit recognized variations not only in personal experiences but also in individuals' ideas about the gods and spirits. There was an "acceptance of personal truths, all considered equally valid when supported by personal experience" (Briggs 1998, 15). The Inuit's openness to the evidence of experience was reflected, in among other ways, by the presence of therapeutic insights in selected Inuit myths.

THE DISEMBOWELER

In self-reports and legends from the Central Canadian Arctic and Greenland, shamans who journeyed to the land on top of the sky frequently had to pass by a spiritual being who was known as the Disemboweler, before they could reach the double house of Brother Moon and Sister Sun (for a detailed ethnography, see Merkur 1992, 277–300). The Disemboweler was almost always a woman, and her appearance was regularly grotesque. Most frequently, her back was hollow and it was possible to see straight through to her spine. When she blocked the path to the moon god's house, she tried to make the approaching shaman laugh by means of grimaces and comic dances. Shamans' tales contained the warning that shamans were not to laugh at her. For example, they were told to pinch the flesh of their thighs surreptitiously to inflict pain that would counter any urge to laugh. If, however, a shaman did laugh at the appearance or antics of the Disemboweler, she would immediately stop her comedy, bring out her *ulo* (woman's knife), and disembowel the laughing shaman. One Baffin Island legend identified her as Brother Moon's wife.

The manifest content of these legends also concealed a secret shamanic teaching. The encounter with the Disemboweler occurred as the manifest content of a vision that was induced by means of sensory deprivation. The visions were technically pseudohallucinations in that they were known to be mental images during their very occurrence. The motif of being disemboweled was the manifest content of a panic attack that might occur during such a vision. By means of the legend, shamans taught apprentice shamans how to manage mood shifts during their visions. They were to control tendencies to slip into hilarity because hilarity might abruptly turn into a panic attack.

The latent content of the shamanic legend is more interesting still. Teasing has extensive use in Inuit child-rearing. The anthropologist Jean L. Briggs (1998), a member of the American Psychoanalytic Association's Interdisciplinary Colloquium, observed that Inuit socialize their children, among other manners, through intensive and prolonged teasing that shifts rapidly between play and seriousness. The teasing requires the children to think about themselves, their social roles, and their desires:

> A way of stimulating children to think and to value ... was to present them with emotionally powerful problems that the children could not ignore. Often this was done by asking a question that was potentially dangerous for the child being

> questioned and dramatizing the consequences of various answers: "Why don't you kill your baby brother?" "Why don't you die so I can have your nice new shirt?" "Your mother's going to die — look, she's cut her finger — do you want to come live with me?" In this way, adults created, or raised to consciousness, issues that the children must have seen as having grave consequences for their lives.
>
> These questions and others equally potent were asked frequently and repetitively in interactions between adults and all small children — especially children between the ages of about two and four. The adult questioners quite consistently perceived themselves, and were perceived by other adults, to be good-humored, benign, and playful.... A large proportion of the interaction between adults and small children consisted of this questioning...
>
> In a sense, this education was a trial by fire. For uninitiated children who were not yet able to understand either the motives of their adult interlocutors or the playful aspect of the questions, the challenge might be severe and the tease a torment. (pp. 5–6)

The approval and disapproval that the children met for their reactions to the teasing taught them that becoming serious is dangerous, while maintaining good humor is socially safe. Children were taught to fear the loss of loved ones, to fear aggression, and to fear being loved too much. The teasing play was highly versatile. Briggs reported the following incident when one child began to realize that he was being teased. "Child utters another cry of protest, but then a fleeting shadow of a smile crosses his face. Adult: '*Now,* he's beginning to just smile!' He resumes his 'attacks' on the child" (Briggs 1990, 35).

One game that Inuit play with children involves a challenge not to smile. A child who is made to smile loses the game, and adults may respond teasingly by frightening the child and pretending to claw him or her (Jean L. Briggs, personal communication, 1998).

Shamans' encounters with the Disemboweler symbolize precisely these predicaments of the Inuit child. The games are games for Inuit adults. For the children, the games are work. Should a child begin to identify with the adults, recognizing a game as "only playing," the adults redouble their efforts, increasing the difficulty of the game to force the child to work once more.

It is most important, I suggest, that the resumption of a game is symbolized in shamanic visions and legends as the manifest visual content of a panic attack. Inuit adults claim that they are only playing, but shamans did not perceive the games as benign. Their visions symbolized them as murderous attacks.

Moreover, shamans were taught to respond differently to the Disemboweler than Inuit children learn to respond to adults. The child's goal is ordinarily to become an adult who considers the games to be playful and amusing. Inuit consider it to be praiseworthy to be always laughing, joking, and playing, "taking nothing seriously" (Briggs 1991a). Briggs emphasized that many valuable individual skills are mastered by shifting from suffering the games to appreciating the amusement of inflicting games on children; however, at the end of the day, what the child learns is to identify with adult aggressors.

The shamanic motif functioned differently. It was precisely the laughter of an adult identifying with the amused aggression of a previous generation that shamans were not to indulge. They instead adopted a different tactic, a different way of relating to teasing, to avoid a panic that was too intense to control through denial or suppression during their alternate states. The shamans' efforts to master their emotions during their visions taught them that the Disemboweler's game was not funny but instead concealed a murderous aggression. They were not to laugh at the Disemboweler, lest she disembowel them. Possibly they imagined that she took offense at being the victim of laughter. The insight that teasing was cruel was both demonstrable and implemented through their experiences of visions. In this manner, they successfully interrupted the unconscious cycle of childhood victimization and adult victimizing, enabling them to work through the traumatic experiences of their childhood.

THE BLIND BOY AND THE LOON

The psychotherapy that Inuit shamans achieved through their visions was available in their societies only to initiated shamans. The therapeutic insights were placed in the public domain, however, in the myths that shamans narrated openly about the moon god. Through the mythology, wholesome insights were made available to children, providing them with guidance. Having detailed the myths elsewhere (Merkur 1991, 174–84), I will here discuss them summarily.

In Alaska, the Western Canadian Arctic, and Greenland, Inuit narrate a tale called "The Blind Boy and the Loon," the protagonist of which is explicitly identified in the central Canadian Arctic as Brother Moon. The story may be summarized as follows. A boy (or young man) lived together with his sister and their mother (or grandmother).

In some versions, he was blind from the start. In most versions, he was a successful hunter who subsequently became blind, in some cases through his mother's malice (which might include witchcraft), but in others by accident. Because he was blind, the family was poor and hungry. One day a bear came to the house and gnawed at the window frame, attempting to enter. The mother aided the boy to aim his bow, which he drew and loosed. He struck the bear, which growled and then died. However, his mother claimed that he had missed the bear and had struck the window frame or the family dog. She then fed herself and her daughter on the bear's meat, while her son went hungry. In some versions, he smelled the meat and was told that he was imagining; in others, he was made to dwell in a separate ice hut away from the smells. In fear of their mother, his sister hid some of the meat in her clothing and brought it to him secretly. The mother was suspicious of the amount of food that the girl claimed to have eaten so very quickly.

In some versions, the brother had the sister guide him to a lake where a loon might be found. In others, the brother called a loon to his ice hut. In most, a loon came to the ice hut on its own initiative. In West and East Greenland, the bird was a wild goose. In any event, the bird took the boy on its back and dove down into a lake. Each time that it dove, the boy's eyesight improved. After two, three, four, or five dives, the boy had not only recovered his eyesight, but become extraordinarily keenly sighted.

The boy returned home. In a few versions, he simply killed his mother outright, but the episode is generally developed more extensively. In some cases, he continued to pretend that he was blind, until he refused to eat the miserable food that his mother served him, giving away his secret. In other cases, he saw the bear skin and his mother had to lie about how she had obtained it. Presently he fashioned hunting weapons and commenced to hunt at the ice edge. His sister might help him, by being tied to the harpoon line and helping him land game. One day his mother offered to help, and she was tied to the harpoon line. White whales (belugas) came by. The boy pretended to aim at a small whale, but he deliberately harpooned one of the largest. His mother was dragged into the sea.

As the mother was dragged beneath the sea by the whale, she would surface periodically and cry out. Some variants have her cry out for a knife, so that she might cut the rope binding her to the whale. In other cases, she reproached her son by speaking of how she had breast fed or diapered him in infancy. In yet other cases, she was resigned to her death. Although some variants end with the mother's disappearance beneath the sea, most have her transformed into either a whale or a narwhal. Several variants specify that she became the first narwhal.

In the Central Canadian Arctic, the blind boy who becomes Brother Moon first becomes a great shaman. No other Inuit deity is ever described as a shaman. Because Inuit shamans always initiated novices in secret, I have elsewhere treated this myth as a secret discussion of shamanic initiation. Here I want to note the object relations. The boy's blindness pertains publicly to the perceptible world of the hunt, and simultaneously alludes secretly to the metaphysics of Inuit gods and spirits. In both cases, the boy is forced by his blindness to cope with an ambiguity that his mother and sister do not experience. The versions that make his mother responsible for his blindness identify the mother as the source of his experience of ambiguity. Although other versions do not blame the mother, Dundes suggests that alternative motifs that have a common narrative function ordinarily pertain to the same unconscious materials. What manifests in one version, is denied in another.

Because Brother Moon and Sister Sun commit incest in a later myth, I treat the sister as a surrogate mother figure, and the doubling of the female characters into mother and sister as a splitting of the mother imago into idealized good and bad mother imagos.

The bear, which the boy kills, is manifestly a game animal; but secretly it is a spirit encountered during shamanic initiations. At both the public and secret levels of the manifest content, the boy attains mastery of the experience. The bear comes to kill him while he is blind and does not know it is coming. With female help, he nevertheless manages to defeat it. There are echoes here of an Oedipal killing of the father, joined together with an incestuous relation with the mother. These Oedipal relations are shaped, however, by the pre-Oedipal mother-child dynamics. The mother induces the ambiguous situation, which the child experiences as blindness and a challenge. However, enough aid is provided despite the ambiguity that the child has a sufficient foundation for creative innovations that permit mastery.

The episode with the bear is consistent, I suggest, with Briggs's (1991b) observations that "Inuit men as well as women often feel very strongly attached to their mothers in a dependent way throughout their lives; and men's love for their wives tends to acquire some of the same character." There are many reasons for this syndrome, including the high rate of loss through death, adoption, and nomadic existence (Briggs 1991a). What I would like to emphasize is the overshadowing of the Oedipus complex by the object-relations of the childhood games.

The emotional difficulty of the achievement of mastery is reflected, among other manners, by the mythic role of the loon. Inuit admired loons for their keen-sightedness, so it was a loon spirit that had the power to heal the boy's blindness. The motif symbolized the adult encouragement that enables a child to carry on with a game of teasing despite its difficulty and distress.

The boy's revenge against his mother externalized his depressiveness as rage against his mother; and it was this same rage, mixed with gratitude, that was directed by hunters against game animals. Once again, I note that in manifesting rather than denying the aggression against the mother, the myth had a therapeutic potential and not merely a symptomatic one.

The woman who became the first narwhal may be compared with the Inuit goddess whom Franz Boas made famous by her Baffin Island name of Sedna. The myth is told that a man wed his daughter to a hunter who was ugly or, in some versions, mistreated her. When the man attempted to fetch his daughter home, her husband pursued, and turned into a great bird whose wings created a storm that threatened to capsize the father's kayak. The father threw his daughter overboard, abandoning her to her husband. When she attempted to hold onto the kayak, he cut her fingers off with the edge of his paddle. The dismembered digits transformed into the sea animals, and the woman became the goddess of the sea. Every hunt at sea was a renewed killing of a part of her body; every meat meal was a feasting on her person. Every period of starvation — a seasonal problem in precontact times — was due to her punitive rage over disobedience to her ritual demands. This portrait of the Mother of the Sea Animals as an abused but abusive woman is, I suggest, to be interpolated in understanding the character of the woman who became a narwhal. Sedna's behavior was not acceptable in an Inuit adult and was strongly discouraged in a child. Its ascription to the great goddess of the sea animals was an instance of making the unconscious conscious.

THE CLAW PEOPLE

In the Canadian Arctic, a few additional tales are told of Brother Moon. The myth of the Claw People begins with the brother and sister wandering about when they came to a village. While the brother built a snow hut, he sent his sister to ask for water because he was thirsty. She went to a house and asked at the window for water for her brother. She was told to enter, but to strip off her jacket to use it to hold the water. When she did so, the people in the house attacked her from behind, using their long, sharp nails. She cried out to her brother for help. He immediately seized a weapon and ran into the house. He killed the claw people, coming at last to an old man, who sat licking flesh and blood from his nails. The old man pleaded that he had warned his children not to attack the girl or her brother would kill them all. The brother killed him as well.

Several versions state that the sister had been badly mauled on her back. Her brother then healed her, except in one Iglulik variant in which the girl recovered naturally. In one variant, she dies and is eaten, so that only her bones remained. Her brother gathered the bones, assembled them, sang over them, and accomplished her resurrection. These acts established the brother as a great shaman.

The myth of the Claw People publicly concerned a category of malicious spirits that were thought to cause illness and death. At its secret level of shamanic innuendo, the death and revival of the sister alluded to shamans' initiatory experiences of panic attacks. In Greenland shamanism, Sister Sun was sometimes said to have a hollow backside that bared her skeleton. More frequently, however, the motif of the hollow backside was attached to the Disemboweler, who was therefore abused as well as abusive. The secret message of the Claw People myth was that the same spirits that induce shamans' panic attacks were responsible for illness, and a shaman who could withstand their attack during his or her initiation had all the power that was necessary to function effectively as a healer.

The latent content of the myth may be compared with the Disemboweler motif. The shamanic experience of a panic attack was portrayed in myth under the symbol of being picked apart with claws that belong not to animals, but to ordinary-looking people in a foreign village. The symbolism offered a significant insight. If strangers clawed at a child as the mother and other caregivers did, one would not hesitate to recognize their behavior as vicious torment. It was only because mothers and other caregivers were idealized in the absence of insight that they came off as well as they did in most Inuit's self-reportage.

THE ORIGIN OF THE VAGINA

The Netsilik and Iglulik Inuit in the Central Canadian Arctic told about another adventure. The brother and sister continued their wandering until they came to a settlement. Outside the houses they saw lumps of good meat, caribou breasts, and rich suet lying about as refuse. The villagers sucked meat, drawing out the juice, but they never swallowed meat because they had no anuses. The brother and sister settled among them, taking spouses. The brother could not consummate his marriage because his wife had no vagina. He took a knife and slit his wife in the crotch, creating one.

In the meantime, his sister became pregnant. Toward the end of her pregnancy, her mother-in-law began to plait caribou sinews into thread. When she entered labor, her mother-in-law sharpened her knife. The older woman intended to cut the infant out of her womb and to sew her up afterward. Her brother intervened, saying that she was not to be slit open because she was able to give birth by herself. Presently she did so, giving birth to a child that had both genitals and an anus. The mother-in-law laughed and sang in delight. She and all the other village women seized meat-forks or other implements and stabbed themselves in the backside. Those that hit the right place gained anuses; those who missed died, the mother-in-law among them.

The religious meaning of the myth pertained to Brother Moon's role to convey souls to wombs, where they reincarnated in fetuses. His activity was the *raison d'être* of the vagina, coitus, and childbirth in all animal species, and so extended to the meat that game animals provided, and the human activities of eating and defecation.

The choice of symbols by which the myth expressed these doctrines is our present concern. The myth resembled, and was a sequel to, the Claw People myth. Like dreams in sequence, it should be interpreted in sequence. Just as the Disemboweler wielded an *ulo* or woman's knife, the mother-in-law seized an *ulo* in preparation for the intended cesarian section. Again, the variable outcome of the concluding attempts to gain an anus was consistent with the variable outcome of a visionary encounter with the Disemboweler. All might be well, or one might die. Furthermore, the mother-in-law laughed before she disemboweled herself, and the Disemboweler made living Inuit laugh before she disemboweled them. Clearly, the character of the mother-in-law was yet an additional presentation of the bad mother imago. It was, however, less purely negative and more ambivalent than previous presentations.

As with the motif of the Disemboweler, we are dealing here not with a symptom of pathology, but with a therapeutic insight in symbolic form. By portraying the mother-in-law's aggression against Sister Sun as unnecessary, the myth asserts the inappropriateness of well-intentioned but uninformed mothering behavior.

To conclude, Brother Moon was portrayed in Inuit myths as singularly resourceful and inventive. He was very much a child who was challenged to figure things out. But it is important not to misrepresent the tone of the interactions. Children chaffed at their mothers and care givers. In chaffing, they were driven to an inventiveness that served them well in dealing with their environment. However, the childhood games of teasing were sufficiently frequently traumatic that at least some Inuit shamans used visions and myths to provide therapeutic insights into the personality dynamics.

Epilogue
CLINICAL IMPLICATIONS

In a famous passage in *New Introductory Lectures on Psycho-Analysis*, Freud (1933) cautioned against reliance on his theory of instincts: "The theory of the instincts is so to say our mythology. Instincts are mythical entities, magnificent in their indefiniteness. In our work, we cannot for a moment disregard them, yet we are never sure that we are seeing them clearly" (p. 95) .

Neither classical psychoanalysts nor Kleinian object relations theorists nor ego psychologists heeded Freud's caution, but the mythological character of the Kleinian system was readily appreciated by its detractors. Robert Wälder (1937), unofficially representing the consensus among psychoanalysts in Vienna, summarized Melanie Klein's theories of early object relations as "the creation of a mythology of the unconscious" in which "the only thing that really exists, or at any rate is worth the analyst's investigation, is the deep unconscious" (p. 467). Wälder's charge that Klein was inventing a new mythology was echoed by S. H. Foulkes, a British analyst, who remarked: "It looks as if we were back at the religious and spiritual level with an independent soul having energies of its own from another world. This is particularly true when these phantasies have attained the dignity of 'inner objects'" (King and Steiner 1991, 364–65).

The characterization of Kleinian theory as a mythology was ignored by most Kleinians until Wilfred R. Bion (1897 to 1979), the most creative and important of the second generation of Kleinians, accepted the attribution. In *Elements of Psycho-Analysis* (1963), Bion defined myth as "the type of statement that philosophers contemptuously dismiss as mythologies when they use the term pejoratively to describe bad theories" (p. 12), but he asserted that he found myths necessary to psychoanalytic work. Bion's (1963, 67) meaning is best conveyed by his reference to "components of the Oedipal myth that ... operated as a pre-conception." Some myths express preconceptions that are present biologically and become inborn knowledge of the breast, parental coitus, and the Oedipus complex. "The myth may be regarded as a primitive form of pre-conception and a stage ... in communication of the individual's private knowledge to his group" (p. 92). Both dreams and myths were vehicles for the expression of preconceptions. "The dream has fresh significance if it is regarded as a private myth" (p. 92). Because all thought is ultimately based in the inborn categories that preconceptions constitute, "the genetic stage of thought is that of dream or myth" (Bion 1965, 29). In Bion's view, the myths that express preconceptions concerned morality, knowledge, and conflict about knowing. With this formulation, Bion implicitly accepted Glover's (1945) charge that Klein's system was mythological because it was ethical, but Bion countered that mythico-ethical thinking is intrinsic to humanity.

For several generations, almost all psychoanalysts subscribed to and worked with Freud's theory of instincts, and object-relations theorists also worked with theories of internal objects that Bion considered mythical. The energy-discharge model postulated vital and mortal forces that were mythical, and object-relations theories credited imagos with a nonexistent autonomy in addition to life and death energies. In neither case did reliance on myths preclude the analysts' effectiveness as healers. The theories contributed to many clinical successes.

HOW ARE WE TO EXPLAIN THE SUCCESSES?

The psychoanalytic myths of instinctual energies and internal objects do not differ from Navajo, Mohave, and Inuit myths in their postulation of indemonstrable, invisible powers or in the effectiveness of the healing that they facilitate. The two psychoanalytic myths always retained contact with reality at an implicitly metaphoric level, as do myths that are conveyed cross-culturally. Freud predicated psychoanalytic theory on a Romantic mythology of vital and mortal energies (Merkur 1993b), but the empiricism of his clinical work permitted several generations of clinicians to achieve positive therapeutic results, despite the mythological character of their axiomatic propositions. Freud's mythology of the instincts and Klein's mythology of internal objects were never sheer fallacies or errors. The theories were ways of talking about empirical clinical phenomena. Analysts who invoked the theories of instinctual energies and internalized objects were unwittingly offering interpretations within the metaphor. The metaphors were at best approximations, but they pertained to realities even when the metaphors were inappropriate, far-fetched, or reified. The theories were never purely speculative, never purely theoretic, never merely fiction. They were always myths.

There is no reason to expect psychoanalysts to function significantly differently in the future. Whatever ideas inform clinical practices in any era will be found erroneous by future generations. The ideas will then be disclosed as metaphors that managed, despite their errors, to refer to real processes. The pertinence of errors to realities inevitably transforms the errors into metaphors. Metaphor is integral to our best creativity. There is inevitably a time lag between the attainment of an innovative metaphor that provides a conceptual breakthrough in human understanding and the subsequent translation of the metaphor into prosaic, discursive language. In addition, people so love metaphors that they often voluntarily forego precise, discursive formulations. The widespread abandonment of the energy-discharge model and the development of relational models without internalized objects have not slaked psychoanalysts' thirst for metaphors. We have instead seen the proliferation of such reified turns of phrase as transitional spaces, disintegrating selves, and analytic thirds.

The plausibility of a clinical interpretation does not and cannot validate a psychoanalytic theory. It can at most show the theory to be tenable. There are no criteria for proving the correctness of an interpretation, either in clinical practice or in the study of myths. In clinical practice, we may evaluate an intervention by the criterion of whether it promotes therapeutic change, but a constructivist epistemology cannot responsibly be avoided. Neither clinical nor applied psychoanalysis has criteria for establishing truth. Our therapeutic techniques rely extensively on reified metaphors. In all cases, the reified metaphors are metaphysical. If theistic, they constitute myths. Though we may try to demythologize as much as we can, myth will always be with us.

Other cultures' myths and healing practices deserve our renewed respect.

REFERENCES

Abraham, Karl. 1909. Dreams and myths: A study in folk-psychology. In *Clinical Papers and Essays on Psycho-Analysis*. Trans. Hilda Abraham and D. R. Ellison. New York: Basic Books, 1955; reprinted New York: Brunner/Mazel, Publishers, 1979.

________. 1922. Two Contributions to the study of symbols. In *Clinical Papers and Essays on Psychoanalysis*, 83–85. Trans. Hilda Abraham and D. R. Ellison. New York: Basic Books, 1955; reprinted New York: Brunner/Mazel, 1979.

Abrams, M. H. 1971. *A Glossary of Literary Terms*. 3rd ed. New York: Holt, Rinehart & Winston.

Adams, Laurie. 1990. The myth of Athena and Arachne: Some Oedipal and pre-Oedipal aspects of creative challenge in women and their implications for the interpretation of *Las Meninas* by Velazquez. *International Journal of Psycho-Analysis* 71:597–609.

Aleksandrowicz, Dov R. 1962. The meaning of metaphor. *Bulletin of the Menninger Clinic* 26:92–101.

Apfelbaum, Bernard. 1966. On ego psychology: A critique of the structural approach to psycho-analytic theory. *International Journal of Psycho-Analysis* 47:451–75.

Arbman, Ernst. 1939. Mythic and religious thought. In *Dragma: Martin P. Nilsson ... Dedicatum*. Lund, Sweden.

Arlow, Jacob A. 1961. Ego psychology and the study of mythology. *Journal of the American Psychoanalytic Association* 9:371–93.

———. 1964. The Madonna's conception through the eyes. *Psychoanalytic Study of Society* 3:13–23.

———. 1969. Unconscious fantasy and disturbances of conscious experience. *Psychoanalytic Quarterly* 38:1–27.

———. 1979. Metaphor and the psychoanalytic situation. *Psychoanalytic Quarterly* 48:363–385.

———. 1981. Discussion of "Apache lore of the bat." In *Psychoanalytic Study of Society*, ed. Werner Muensterberger and L. Bryce Boyer, 9:313–17. New York: Psychohistory Press.

Arlow, Jacob A., and Brenner, Charles. 1964. *Psychoanalytic Concepts and the Structural Hypothesis*. New York: International Universities Press.

Badcock, C. R. 1980. *The Psychoanalysis of Culture*. Oxford: Basil Blackwell.

Bakan, David. 1979. *And They Took Themselves Wives: The Emergence of Patriarchy in Western Civilization*. San Francisco: Harper & Row.

Balikci, Asen. 1963. Shamanistic behavior among the Netsilik Eskimo. *Southwestern Journal of Anthropology* 19:380–96.

Barbour, Ian G. 1974. *Myths, Models, and Paradigms: A Comparative Study in Science and Religion*. New York: Harper & Row.

Barnouw, Victor. 1955. A psychological interpretation of a Chippewa origin legend. *Journal of American Folk-Lore* 68:73–85, 211–23, 341–55.

Bascom, William R. 1965. The forms of folklore: Prose narratives. *Journal of American Folk-Lore* 78 (307):3–20.

Baudry, Francis. 1988. From prophet to poet: Jacob A. Arlow's contributions to applied psychoanalysis. In *Fantasy, Myth, and Reality: Essays in Honor of Jacob A. Arlow, M.D.*, ed. Harold P. Blum, Yale Kramer, Arlene K. Richards, and Arnold D. Richards, 41–58. Madison, CT: International Universities Press.

Beres, David. 1965. Symbol and object. *Bulletin of the Menninger Clinic* 29:3–23.

Bion, Wilfred R. 1963. *Elements of Psycho-Analysis*. New York: Basic Books, Inc.

———. 1965. *Transformations*. London: William Heinemann Medical Books Ltd; reprinted London: Karnac, 1984.

Birket-Smith, Kaj. 1924. Ethnography of the Egedesminde district. *Meddelelser om Grønland* Vol. 66 København. Reitzel. Reprinted New York AMS Press, 1976.

———. 1953. *The Chugach Eskimo*. Nationalmuseets Skrifter, Ethnografisk Roekke 6. Copenhagen: Nationalmuseets Publikationsfond.

———. 1959. *The Eskimos*. 2nd ed. London: Methuen & Co. Ltd.

Blum, Harold P. 1988. A tribute to Jacob A. Arlow, M.D. In *Fantasy, Myth, and Reality: Essays in Honor of Jacob A. Arlow, M.D.*, ed. Harold P. Blum, Yale Kramer, Arlene K. Richards, and Arnold D. Richards, 3–8. Madison, CT: International Universities Press.

Boas, Franz. 1888. *The Central Eskimo. Annual Report of the Bureau of American Ethnology*, 6:399–669. Reprinted Toronto: Coles Publishing Co., 1974.

———. 1894. Notes on the Eskimo of Port Clarence, Alaska. *Journal of American Folk-Lore* 7:205–8.

———. 1901. The Eskimo of Baffin Land and Hudson Bay. *American Museum of Natural History, Bulletin* 15(1)

———. 1904. The folk-lore of the Eskimo. *Journal of American Folk-Lore* 17:1–13.

———. 1907. Second report on the Eskimo of Baffin Land and Hudson Bay. *American Museum of Natural History, Bulletin*, Vol. 15, Part 2.

Borbely, Antal F. 1998. A psychoanalytic concept of metaphor. *International Journal of Psycho-Analysis* 79:923–36.

Bowker, John. 1973. *The Sense of God: Sociological, Anthropological and Psychological Approaches to the Origin of the Sense of God*. Oxford: Clarendon Press.

Boyer, L. Bryce. 1964. An example of legend distortion from the Apaches of the Mescalero Indian reservation. *Journal of American Folk-Lore* 77:118–42.

———. 1977. Mythology, folklore, and psychoanalysis. In *International Encyclopedia of Psychiatry, Psychology, Psychoanalysis, and Neurology*. Vol. 7, ed. Benjamin B. Wolman, 423–429. New York: Aesculapius Publishers and Van Nostrand.

———. 1981. Psychoanalysis, folklore and socialization processes (A Panel Discussion of the American Psychoanalytic Association, Baltimore, May 1976) Introductory remarks. In *Psychoanalytic Study of Society*, ed. Werner Muensterberger and L. Bryce Boyer, 9:257–62. New York: Psychohistory Press.

Boyer, Ruth M., and L. Bryce Boyer. 1981. Apache lore of the bat. In *Psychoanalytic Study of Society*, ed. Werner Muensterberger and L. Bryce Boyer, 9:263–299. New York: Psychohistory Press.

Brenner, Arthur B. 1950. The great mother goddess: Puberty initiation rites and the covenant of Abraham. *Psychoanalytic Review* 37:320–40.

Brenner, Charles. 1982. *The Mind in Conflict*. New York: International Universities Press.

Briggs, Jean L. 1990. Playwork as a tool in the socialization of an Inuit child. *Arctic Medical Research* 49:34–38.

———. 1991a. Expecting the unexpected: Canadian Inuit training for an experimental lifestyle. *Ethos* 19:259–87.

———. 1991b. Mazes of meaning: The exploration of individuality in culture and of culture through individual constructs. *The Psychoanalytic Study of Society* Vol. 16, ed. L. Bryce Boyer and Ruth M. Boyer, 111–53. Hillsdale, NJ: Analytic Press.

———. 1998. *Inuit Morality Play: The Emotional Education of a Three-Year-Old.* New Haven and London: Yale University Press.

Brown, Joseph Epes. 1979. The immediacy of the mythological message: Native American traditions. In *Native Religious Traditions.* In ed. Earl H. Waugh and K. Dad Prithipaul. Waterloo: Wilfrid Laurier University Press, 1979.

Bultmann, Rudolf. 1953. New Testament and mythology. In *Kerygma and Myth: A Theological Debate.* New York: Harper & Row, 1961.

Burrows, Elizabeth. 1926. Eskimo tales. *Journal of American Folk-Lore* 39:79–81.

Cain, Albert C., and Barbara M. Maupin. 1961. Interpretation within the metaphor. *Bulletin of the Menninger Clinic* 25:307–11.

Caldwell, Richard. 1990. The psychoanalytic interpretation of Greek myth. In *Approaches to Greek Myth*, ed. Lowell Edmunds, 344–89. Baltimore and London: Johns Hopkins University Press.

Campbell, Joseph. 1959–1968. *The Masks of God.* 4 vols. New York: Viking Press.

Carpenter, Edwin S. 1955. Changes in the Sedna myth among the Aivilik. *Anthropological Papers of the University of Alaska* 3(2) :69–74.

———. 1956. The timeless present in the mythology of the Aivilik Eskimos. *Anthropologica* 3:1–4.

Caruth, Elaine, and Rudolf Ekstein. 1966. Interpretation within the metaphor: Further considerations. *Journal of the American Academy of Child Psychiatry* 5:35–46. Reprinted in Rudolf Ekstein. *Children of Time and Space, of Action and Impulse: Clinical Studies on the Psychoanalytic Treatment of Severely Disturbed Children*, 158–65. New York: Appleton-Century-Crofts, 1966.

Cassirer, Ernst. 1955. *The Philosophy of Symbolic Forms. Vol. II: Mythical Thought.* Trans. Ralph Manheim. New Haven: Yale University Press.

Cox, Howard L. 1948. The place of mythology in the study of culture. *American Imago* 5:83–94.

Curtis, Edward S. 1930. *The North American Indian.* Vol. 20, Seattle, WA: E.S. Curtis. Reprinted New York: Johnson Reprint Corporation, 1970.

Devereux, George. 1939. Maladjustment and social neurosis. *American Sociological Review* 4:844–851.

———. 1948. Mohave coyote tales. *Journal of American Folklore* 61(241) :233–55.

———. 1953a. Géza Róheim 1891–1953. *American Anthropologist* 55(3) :420.

———. 1953b. Why Oedipus killed Laius: A note on the complementary Oedipus complex in Greek drama. *International Journal of Psycho-Analysis* 34:132–41.

———. 1957. The criteria of dual competence in psychiatric-anthropological studies. *Journal of the Hillside Hospital* 6:87–90.

———. 1958. Cultural thought models in primitive and modern psychiatric theories. *Psychiatry* 21:359–74.

———. 1961. Shamans as neurotics. *American Anthropologist* 63:1088–91.

———. 1970. Normal and abnormal: The key concepts of ethnopsychiatry. In *Man and His Culture: Psychoanalytic Anthropology after 'Totem and Taboo,'* ed. Warner Muensterberger, 113–36. New York: Taplinger Publishing Company.

Dorson, Richard M. 1955. The eclipse of solar mythology. In *Myth: A Symposium*, ed. Thomas A. Sebeok. Bloomington: Indiana University Press, 1965.

Ducey, Charles. 1976. The life history and creative psychopathology of the shaman: Ethnopsychoanalytic perspectives. *Psychoanalytic Study of Society* 7:173–230.

———. 1979. The shaman's dream journey: Psychoanalytic and structural complementarity in myth interpretation. *Psychoanalytic Study of Society* 8:71–117.
Dundes, Alan. 1962. From emic to etic units in the structural study of folktales. *Journal of American Folk-Lore* 75:95–105. Reprinted in Dundes. *Analytic Essays in Folklore*, 61–72. The Hague: Mouton Publishers, 1975.
———. 1964. Texture, text, and context. *Southern Folklore Quarterly* 28:251–65. Reprinted in *Essays in Folkloristics*. Meerut, India: Folklore Institute, 1978.
———. 1966. Metafolklore and oral literary criticism. *The Monist* 50:505–16. Reprinted in Dundes. *Analytic Essays in Folklore*. The Hague: Mouton Publishers, 1975.
———. 1971. Folk ideas as units of worldview. *Journal of American Folk-Lore* 84:93–103. Reprinted in Dundes. *Essays in Folkloristics*. Meerut, India: Folklore Institute, 1978.
———. 1975. *Analytic Essays in Folklore*. The Hague: Mouton.
———. 1980. *Interpreting Folklore*. Bloomington: Indiana University Press, 1980.
———. 1981. Discussion of "Apache lore of the bat." *Psychoanalytic Study of Society*, ed. Werner Muensterberger and L. Bryce Boyer, 9:301–12. New York: Psychohistory Press.
———. 1984. *Life is Like a Chicken Coop Ladder: A Portrait of German Culture Through Folklore*. New York: Columbia University Press.
———. 1987. *Parsing Through Customs: Essays by a Freudian Folklorist*. Madison: University of Wisconsin Press.
———. 1992. Introduction. In Géza Róheim. *Fire in the Dragon: and Other Psychoanalytic Essays on Folklore*. ed. Alan Dundes, ix–xxvi. Princeton: Princeton University Press, 1992.
———. 1997a. *From Game to War: and Other Psychoanalytic Essays on Folklore*. Lexington, KY: University Press of Kentucky.
———. 1997b. *Two Tales of Crow and Sparrow: A Freudian Folkloristic Essay on Caste and Untouchability*. Lanham, MD: Rowman & Littlefield.
Eagle, Morris N. 1984. *Recent Developments in Psychoanalysis: A Critical Evaluation*. Cambridge, MA: Harvard University Press.
Edmunds, Lowell. 1985. *Oedipus: The Ancient Legend and Its Later Analogues*. Baltimore: Johns Hopkins University Press.
Edmunds, Lowell, and Alan Dundes, eds. 1984. *Oedipus: A Folklore Casebook*. New York and London: Garland Publishing.
Eggan, Dorothy. 1955. The personal use of myth in dreams. *Journal of American Folk-Lore* 68:445–53.
Eisenstein, Samuel. 1966. Otto Rank 1884–1939: The myth of the birth of the hero. In *Psychoanalytic Pioneers*, ed. Franz Alexander, Samuel Eisenstein, and Martin Grotjahn, 36–50. New York: Basic Books.
Ekstein, Rudolf, and Judith Wallerstein. 1956. Observations on the psychotherapy of borderline and psychotic children. *Psychoanalytic Study of the Child* 11:303–11. Reprinted in Rudolf Ekstein. *Children of Time and Space, of Action and Impulse: Clinical Studies on the Psychoanalytic Treatment of Severely Disturbed Children*, 148–57. New York: Appleton-Century-Crofts, 1966.
Eliade, Mircea. 1960. *Myths, Dreams, and Mysteries: The Encounter Between Contemporary Faiths and Archaic Realities*. Trans. Philip Mairet. New York: Harper & Row.
———. 1963. *Myth and Reality*. Trans. Willard R. Trask. New York: Harper & Row.
Fairbairn, W. Ronald D. 1963. Synopsis of an object-relations theory of the personality. *International Journal of Psycho-Analysis* 44:224225.
Feldman, Burton, and Robert D. Richardson. 1972. *The Rise of Modern Mythology 1680–1860*. Bloomington: Indiana University Press, 1975.
Fenichel, Otto. 1945. *The Psychoanalytic Theory of Neurosis*. New York: W. W. Norton & Co., Inc.

Ferenczi, Sándor. 1912. The symbolic representation of the pleasure and reality principles in the Oedipus myth. In *First Contributions to Psycho-Analysis*. 1916; reprinted New York: Brunner/Mazel, 1980.
———. 1933. Thalassa: A theory of genitality. *Psychoanalytic Quarterly* 2:361–403.
Ferenczi, Sándor, and Rank, Otto. 1923. *The Development of Psycho-Analysis*. Trans. Caroline Newton. New Tork: Nervous and Mental Disease Publishing Co., 1925. Reprinted New York: Dover Publications, Inc., 1956.
Fisher, John F. 1975. An analysis of the Central Eskimo Sedna myth. *Temenos* 11:27–42.
Fliess, Robert. 1973. *Symbol, Dream, and Psychosis*. New York: International Universities Press, Inc.
Flügel, J. C. 1924. Polyphallic symbolism and the castration complex. *International Journal of Psycho-Analysis* 5:155–96.
Frederiksen, Svend. 1954. Stylistic forms in Greenland Eskimo literature. *Meddelelser om Grønland*, Vol. 136, No. 7. København: C. A. Reitzel.
Freeman, Daniel M. A. 1981. Mythological portrayal of developmental processes and major intrapsychic restructuralizations. In *Psychoanalytic Study of Society*, ed. Werner Muensterberger and L. Bryce Boyer, 9:319–40. New York: Psychohistory Press.
French, Thomas M., and Erika Fromm. 1964. *Dream Interpretation: A New Approach*. New York: Basic Books; reprinted Madison, CT: International Universities Press, 1986.
Freuchen, Peter. 1935. *Arctic Adventures: My Life in the Frozen North*. New York: Farrar & Rinehart.
———. 1961. *Book of the Eskimos*. Cleveland: World Publishing Company.
Freud, Anna. 1966. *The Ego and the Mechanisms of Defense*. 2nd ed. New York: International Universities Press, 1980.
Freud, Sigmund. 1900. The interpretation of dreams. In *The Standard Edition of the Complete Psychological Works of Sigmund Freud*, ed. James Strachey, with Anna Freud, Alix Strachey, and Alan Tyson, 4–5. London: Hogarth Press, 1958.
———. 1901a. On dreams. In *Standard Edition* 5:633–86. London: Hogarth Press, 1958.
———. 1901b. The psychopathology of everyday life. In *Standard Edition* 6:1–279. London: Hogarth Press, 1960.
———. 1905. Three essays on the theory of sexuality. In *Standard Edition* 7:130–243. London: Hogarth Press, 1953.
———. 1908. Character and anal erotism. In *Standard Edition* 9:169–175. London: Hogarth Press, 1959.
———. 1909. Analysis of a phobia in a five-year-old boy. In *Standard Edition* 10:5–149. London: Hogarth Press, 1955.
———. 1910a. Five lectures on psycho-analysis. In *Standard Edition* 11:9–55. London: Hogarth Press, 1957.
———. 1910b. Leonardo da Vinci and a memory of his childhood. In *Standard Edition* 11:63–137. London: Hogarth Press, 1957.
———. 1911. Formulations on the two principles of mental functioning. In *Standard Edition* 12:218–26. London: Hogarth Press, 1958.
———. 1913. Totem and taboo: Some points of agreement between the mental life of savages and neurotics. In *Standard Edition*, 13:1–161. London: Hogarth Press, 1958.
———. 1914. On the history of the psycho-analytic movement. In *Standard Edition* 14:7–66. London: Hogarth Press, 1957.
———. 1916–17. Introductory lectures on psycho-analysis. In *Standard Edition* 15–16:9–463. London: Hogarth Press, 1961–1963.
———. 1920. Beyond the pleasure principle. In *Standard Edition* 18:7–64. London: Hogarth Press, 1955.
———. 1921. Group psychology and the analysis of the ego. In *Standard Edition* 18:69–143. London: Hogarth Press, 1955.

———. 1922. Dreams and telepathy. In *Standard Edition* 18:197–220. London: Hogarth Press, 1955.
———. 1923a. The ego and the id. In *Standard Edition* 19:12–59. London: Hogarth Press, 1961.
———. 1923b. Remarks on the theory and practice of dream interpretation. In *Standard Edition* 19:109–21. London: Hogarth Press, 1961.
———. 1925. An autobiographical study. In *Standard Edition* 20:7–74. London: Hogarth Press, 1959.
———. 1926a. Inhibitions, symptoms, and anxiety. In *Standard Edition*, 20:87–172. London: Hogarth Press, 1959.
———. 1926b. The question of lay analysis: Conversations with an impartial person. In *Standard Edition* 20:183–258. London: Hogarth Press, 1959.
———. 1930. Civilization and its discontents. In *Standard Edition* 21:64–145. London: Hogarth Press, 1961.
———. 1933. New introductory lectures on psycho-analysis. In *Standard Edition* 22:5–182. London: Hogarth Press, 1964.
———. 1937. Analysis terminable and interminable. In *Standard Edition* 23:216–53. London: Hogarth Press, 1964.
———. 1940a. Medusa's head. In *Standard Edition* 18:273–74. London: Hogarth Press, 1955.
———. 1940b. An outline of psycho-analysis. In *Standard Edition* 23:144–207. London: Hogarth Press, 1964.
———. 1985. *The Complete Letters of Sigmund Freud to Wilhelm Fliess, 1887–1904.* Trans. Jeffrey Moussaieff Masson. Cambridge, MA: Belknap Press of Harvard University Press.
Frieden, Ken. 1990. *Freud's Dream of Interpretation*. Albany: State University of New York Press.
Frisbie, Charlotte Johnson. 1967. *Kinaalda: A Study of the Navajo Girl's Puberty Ceremonial.* Middleton, CT: Wesleyan University Press.
Fromm, Erich. 1944. Individual and social origins of neurosis. *American Sociological Review* 9:380–384; reprinted in: *Personality in Nature, Society, and Culture*, Clyde Kluckhohn and Henry A. Murray, eds., 407–13. New York: Alfred A. Knopf, 1948.
———. 1959. The Oedipus complex and the Oedipus myth. In Ruth Nanda Anshen, ed., *The Family: Its Function and Destiny.* 2nd ed. New York: Harper & Row.
Gillham, C. E. 1955. *Medicine Men of Hooper Bay, or The Eskimo's Arabian Nights*. London: The Batchworth Press.
Glover, Edward. 1945. Examination of the Klein system of child psychology. *Psychoanalytic Study of the Child* 1:75–118.
Goldenweiser, Alexander A. 1910. Totemism, an analytical study. *Journal of American Folk-Lore* 23:179–293.
Graber, G. H. 1952. Der Sohn-Komplex der Väter. *Der Psychologe* 4:250–58.
Green, André. 1986. *On Private Madness*. London: Hogarth Press, and Madison, CT: International Universities Press.
Grossman, Lee. 1993. The significance of religious themes and fantasies during psychoanalysis. *Journal of the American Psychoanalytic Association* 41:755–64.
Grotjahn, Martin. 1966. Karl Abraham 1877–1925: The first German psychoanalyst. In *Psychoanalytic Pioneers*, ed. Franz Alexander, Samuel Eisenstein, and Martin Grotjahn, 1–13. New York: Basic Books.
Gubser, Nicholas J. 1965. *The Nunamiut Eskimos: Hunters of Caribou*. New Haven: Yale University Press.
Guthrie, Thomas C. 1955. Oedipus myth in ancient Greece. *Psychiatric Quarterly* 29:543–554.

Haile, Berard. 1943. Soul concepts of the Navaho. *Annali Lateranensi* 7:61–94.
———. 1978. *Love-Magic and Butterfly People: The Slim Curly Version of the Ajilee and Mothway Myths.* Flagstaff: Museum of Northern Arizona Press.
Hamilton, N. Gregory. 1980. The trickster: The use of folklore in psychoanalytic psychotherapy. *Bulletin of the Menninger Clinic* 44(4) :364–80.
———. 1990. *Self and Others: Object Relations Theory in Practice.* Northvale, NJ: Jason Aronson.
Harrison, Jane. 1955. *Prolegomena to the Study of Greek Religion.* New York: Meridian Books.
Hartmann, Heinz. 1939. *Ego Psychology and the Problem of Adaptation.* New York: International Universities Press, 1958.
Hawkes, Ernest W. 1916. *The Labrador Eskimo.* Canada Department of Mines, Geological Survey, Memoir 91. No. 14, Anthropological Series. Ottawa: Government Printing Bureau. New York: Johnson Reprint Corporation, 1970.
Hesse, Mary. 1970. *Models and Analogies in Science.* Notre Dame: Notre Dame University Press, 1970.
Hill, W. W. 1938a. The agricultural and hunting methods of the Navaho Indians. *Yale University Publications in Anthropology*, no. 18.
———. 1938b. Navajo use of jimsonweed. *New Mexico Anthropologist* 3(2) :19–21.
Hodgkins, Gael. 1977. Sedna: Images of the transcendent in an Eskimo goddess. In *Beyond Androcentrism: New Essays on Women and Religion*, ed. Rita M. Gross. Missoula, MT: Scholars Press.
Holm, Gustav. 1912. Legends and tales from Angmagsalik. *Meddeleser om Grønland* Vol. 136, No. 7. København: C. A. Reitzel.
Holtved, Erik. 1951. The Polar Eskimos: Language and folklore. II. Myths and tales translated. *Meddelelser om Grønland* Vol. 152, No. 2. København: C. A. Reitzel.
———. 1966–1967. The Eskimo myth about the sea-woman. A folkloristic sketch. *Folk* 8/9:145–53.
———. 1974–1975. Myth collecting in Greenland and Alaska. *Folk* 16/17:15–24.
Honko, Lauri. 1972. The problem of defining myth. In *The Myth of the State*, ed. Haralds Biezais. Stockholm: Almqvist & Wiksell.
Hultkrantz, Åke. 1965. Les réligions du Grand Nord Americain. In *Les Réligions Arctiques et Finnoises: Siberiens—Finnois—Lapons—Esquimaux*, ed. Ivar Paulson, Âke Hultkrantz, and Karl Jettmar. Paris: Payot.
———. 1972. An ideological dichotomy: Myths and folk beliefs among the Shoshoni Indians of Wyoming. *History of Religions* 11(4) :339–53.
———. 1973. A definition of shamanism. *Temenos* 9:25–37.
———. 1979. Myths in Native North American religions. In *Native Religious Traditions*, ed. Earl H. Waugh and K. Dad Prithipaul. Waterloo: Wilfrid Laurier University Press.
Ingram, John. 1963. Malinowski: Epistemology and Oedipus. *Kroeber Anthropological Society Papers* 29:1–14.
Isaacs, Susan. 1948. The nature and function of phantasy. *International Journal of Psycho-Analysis* 29:73–97.
Jacobs, Melville. 1952. Psychological inferences from a Chinook myth. *Journal of American Folk-Lore* 65:121–37.
Jenness, Diamond. 1922. *The Life of the Copper Eskimos.* Ottowa, Canada: King's Printer. Reprinted New York: Johnson Reprint Corporation, 1970.
———. 1926. *Myths and Traditions from Northern Alaska, The Mackenzie Delta, and Coronation Gulf.* Report of the Canadian Arctic Expedition 1913–18. Vol. 13, Part A. Ottawa: F. A. Acland.
———. 1941. The Carrier Indians of the Bulkley River: Their social and religious life. *Bureau of American Ethnology, Bulletin* 133

Jensen, Adolf E. 1963. *Myth and Cult Among Primitive Peoples.* Trans. Marianna Tax Choldin and Wolfgang Weissleder. Chicago: University of Chicago Press.

Johnson, Allen W., and Douglass Price-Williams, eds. 1996. *Oedipus Ubiquitous: The Family Complex in World Folk Literature.* Stanford, CA: Stanford University Press.

Jones, Ernest. 1916. The theory of symbolism. In Jones, *Papers on Psycho–Analysis.* 5th ed. 87–144. London: Bailliere, Tindall & Cox, 1948.

———. 1928. Psycho-analysis and folklore. In jones, *Essays in Applied Psycho-Analysis, Vol. II: Essays in Folklore, Anthropology and Religion.* 1–21. London: Hogarth Press Ltd., 1951.

———. 1931. *On the Nightmare.* 2nd ed. New York: Liveright Publishing Corporation, 1951.

Jung, Carl Gustav. 1973. *Memories, Dreams, Reflections*, ed. Aniela Jaffe. 2nd ed. Trans. Richard and Clara Winston. Reprinted New York: Vintage Books/Random House, 1989.

Kanzer, Mark. 1948. The 'passing of the Oedipus complex' in Greek drama. *International Journal of Psycho-Analysis* 29:131–34.

———. 1964. On interpreting the Oedipus plays. *Psychoanalytic Study of Society* 3:26–38.

Kaplan, Bert, and Dale Johnson. 1964. The social meaning of Navaho psychopathology and psychotherapy. In *Magic, Faith, and Healing: Studies in Primitive Psychiatry Today*, ed. Ari Kiev, 203–29. New York: Free Press, 1964.

Kardiner, Abram. 1939. *The Individual and His Society: The Psychodynamics of Primitive Social Organization.* New York: Columbia University Press.

———. 1956. Adaptational theory: The cross cultural point of view. In *Changing Concepts of Psychoanalytic Medicine*, eds. Sandor Rado and George E. Daniels, 59–68. New York and London: Grune & Stratton.

———. 1959. Social and cultural implications of psychoanalysis. In *Psychoanalysis, Scientific Method, and Philosophy: A Symposium*, ed. Sidney Hook, 81–103. New York: New York University Press.

Kardiner, Abram, with Ralph Linton, Cora Du Bois, and James West. 1945. *The Psychological Frontiers of Society.* New York: Columbia University Press.

Kausen, Rudolf. 1972. Laius complex and mother-child symbiosis. *Journal of Individual Psychology* 28:33–37.

———. 1973. More on the Laius complex. *Journal of Individual Psychology* 29:88–91.

King, Pearl and Riccardo Steiner. 1991. *The Freud-Klein Controversies 1941–1945.* London and New York: Tavistock Routledge.

Kirk, G. S. 1974. *The Nature of Greek Myths.* Harmondsworth: U.K., Penguin Books Ltd., 1974.

Klein, Melanie. 1930. The importance of symbol-formation in the development of the ego. *International Journal of Psycho-Analysis* 11:24–39. Reprinted in Klein. *Love, Guilt and Reparation and Other Works 1921–1945*, 219–32. New York: Delacorte Press, 1975.

Kluckhohn, Clyde. 1938. Participation in ceremonials in a Navaho community. *American Anthropologist* 40:359–69.

———. 1942. Myths and rituals: A general theory. *Harvard Theological Review* 35:45–79.

———. 1944. *Navaho Witchcraft.* Cambridge Peabody Museum. Reprinted Boston: Beacon Press, 1967.

Kluckhohn, Clyde, and Dorothea Leighton. 1974. *The Navaho.* 2nd ed. Garden City, NY: Natural History Library, 1962; reprinted Cambridge: Harvard University Press.

Kohut, Heinz. 1971. *The Analysis of the Self: A Systematic Approach to the Psychoanalytic Treatment of Narcissistic Personality Disorders.* Madison, CT: International Universities Press.

———. 1977. *The Restoration of the Self.* New York: International Universities Press.

———. 1984. *How Does Analysis Cure?* ed. Arnold Goldberg with Paul Stepansky. Chicago: University of Chicago Press.

Kopp, Richard R. 1995. *Metaphor Therapy: Using Client-Generated Metaphors in Psychotherapy.* New York: Brunner/Mazel.

Koppers, Wilhelm. 1930. Der Hund in der Mythologie der zirkumpazifischen Volker: Ein Beitrag zür Frage der alt-neuweltlichen Kulturbeziehungen. *Wiener Beitrage zür Kulturgeschichte und Linguistik* 1:359–99.

Kramer, Yale. 1988. In the visions of the night: Perspectives on the work of Jacob A. Arlow. In *Fantasy, Myth, and Reality: Essays in Honor of Jacob A. Arlow, M.D.*, ed. Harold P. Blum, Yale Kramer, Arlene K. Richards, and Arnold D. Richards, 9–39. Madison, CT: International Universities Press.

Kretschmar, Freda. 1938. *Hundestammvater und Kerberos.* 2 vols. Stuttgart: Strecker und Schroder Verlag.

Kris, Ernst. 1934. The psychology of caricature. Reprinted in Kris. *Psychoanalytic Exploration in Art*, 173–88. New York: International Universities Press, 1952.

Kroeber, Alfred Louis. 1899. Tales of the Smith Sound Eskimo. *Journal of American Folk-Lore* 12:166–83.

La Barre, Weston. 1948. Folklore and psychology. *Journal of American Folk-Lore* 61:382–90.

———. 1959. Religions, Rorschachs, and tranquilizers. *American Journal of Orthopsychiatry* 29:688–98.

———. 1960. Neurotic defense mechanisms in supernatural religion. *The Humanist* 6:323–31.

———. 1966. Geza Roheim. In *Psychoanalytic Pioneers*, ed. Franz Alexander, Samuel Eisenstein, and Martin Grotjahn, 272–81. New York: Basic Books.

Lakoff, George. 1987. *Women, Fire, and Dangerous Things: What Categories Reveal about the Mind.* Chicago: University of Chicago Press.

———. 1993. The contemporary theory of metaphor. In *Metaphor and Thought.* 2nd ed., ed. Andrew Ortony, 202–51. Cambridge: University Press.

Lakoff, George, and Mark Johnson. 1980. *Metaphors We Live By.* Chicago: University of Chicago Press.

———. 1999. *Philosophy in the Flesh: The Embodied Mind and Its Challenge to Western Thought.* New York: Basic Books.

Lakoff, George, and Mark Turner. 1989. *More than Cool Reason: A Field Guide to Poetic Metaphor.* Chicago: University of Chicago Press.

Lamberton, Robert. 1986. *Homer the Theologian: Neoplatonist Allegorical Reading and the Growth of the Epic Tradition.* Berkeley: University of California Press.

Lancaster, Elizabeth. 1932. Sex and complex: Oedipus or Kronos? *Man* 32:151–52.

Langer, Susanne K. 1957. *Philosophy in a New Key: A Study in the Symbolism of Reason, Rite, and Art.* 3rd ed. Cambridge, MA: Harvard University Press.

Lantis, Margaret. 1938. The mythology of Kodiak Island, Alaska. *Journal of American Folk-Lore* 51:123–72.

———. 1946. The social culture of the Nunivak Eskimo. *Transactions of the American Philosophical Society*, Vol. 35, Part 3.

Lazarsfeld, Sofie. 1944. Did Oedipus have an Oedipus complex? *American Journal of Orthopsychiatry* 14:226–29.

Leatherdale, W. H. 1974. *The Role of Analogy, Model, and Metaphor in Science.* Amsterdam and New York: American Elsevier.

Leavy, Stanley A. 1973. Psychoanalytic interpretation. *Psychoanalytic Study of the Child* 28:305–30.

Leenhardt, Maurice. 1979. *Do Kamo: Person and Myth in the Melanesian World.* Trans. Basia Miller Gulati. Chicago: University of Chicago Press.

Levin, A. J. 1948. The Oedipus myth in history and psychiatry: A new interpretation. *Psychiatry* 11:283299.

———. 1957. Oedipus and Samson: The rejected hero-child. *International Journal of Psycho-Analysis* 38:105–16.

Levy-Bruhl, Lucien. 1923. *Primitive Mentality.* Trans. Lilian A. Clare. New York: AMS Press, 1978.

———. 1926. *How Natives Think*. Trans. Lilian A. Clare. London: Allen. Reprinted New York: Arno Press, 1979.

Lewin, Bertram D. 1952. Phobic symptoms and dream interpretation. *Psychoanalytic Quarterly* 21:295–322.

Lidz, Theodore. 1988. The riddle of the riddle of the Sphinx. *Psychoanalytic Review* 75(1):35–49.

Lindén, Jitka. 1985. Insight through metaphor in psychotherapy and creativity. *Psychoanalysis and Contemporary Thought* 8(3) :375–406.

Lisiansky, Urey. 1814. *Voyage Round the World in the Years 1803, 1804, 1805, and 1806.* Ridgewood, NJ: Gregg Press, 1968.

Luckert, Karl W. 1975. *The Navajo Hunter Tradition.* Tucson: University of Arizona Press.

———. 1978. *A Navajo Bringing-Home Ceremony: The Claus Chee Sonny Version of Deerway Ajilee.* Flagstaff: Museum of Northern Arizona Press.

———. 1979. *Coyoteway: A Navajo Holyway Healing Ceremonial.* Tucson: University of Arizona Press.

MacCormac, Earl R. 1976. *Metaphor and Myth in Science and Religion.* Durham: Duke University Press.

Malaurie, Jean. 1982. *The Last Kings of Thule: With the Polar Eskimos, As They Face Their Destiny.* New York: E. P. Dutton, Inc.

Malinowski, Bronislaw. 1924. Psycho-analysis and anthropology. *Psyche* 4:293–332.

———. 1926. Myth in primitive psychology. In Malinowski. *Magic, Science and Religion: and Other Essays.* New York: Doubleday Anchor Books, 1954.

———. 1927. *Sex and Repression in Savage Society.* London: Kegan Paul.

Maslow, Abraham H. 1970. *Motivation and Personality.* 3rd ed. New York: HarperCollins.

Matthews, Washington. 1902. *The Night Chant, A Navaho Ceremony. American Museum of Natural History, Memoirs* Vol. 6, Part 5. Reprinted New York: AMS Press, 1978.

May, Rollo. 1961. The meaning of the Oedipus myth. *Review of Existential Psychology and Psychiatry* 1:44–52.

Melnick, Burton A. 1997. Metaphor and the theory of libidinal development. *International Journal of Psycho-Analysis* 78:997–1015.

Merkur, Dan. 1991. *Powers Which We Do Not Know: The Gods and Spirits of the Inuit.* Moscow, ID: University of Idaho Press.

———. 1992. *Becoming Half Hidden: Shamanism and Initiation Among the Inuit.* 2nd ed. New York and London: Garland Publications.

———. 1993a. *Gnosis: An Esoteric Tradition of Mystical Visions and Unions.* Albany: State University of New York Press.

———. 1993b. Mythology into metapsychology: Freud's misappropriation of Romanticism. In *The Psychoanalytic Study of Society.* ed. L. Bryce Boyer, Ruth M. Boyer, and Stephen M. Sonnenberg, 18:345–60. Hillsdale, NJ: Analytic Press.

———. 1999. *Mystical Moments and Unitive Thinking.* Albany: State University of New York Press.

———. 2001. *Unconscious Wisdom: A Superego Function in Dreams, Conscience, and Inspiration.* Albany: State University of New York Press.

———. 2002. The Ojibwa vision quest. *Journal of Applied Psychoanalytic Studies* 4(2):149–70.

Michels, Robert. 1986. Oedipus and insight. *Psychoanalytic Quarterly* 55:599–617. Reprinted in *The Oedipus Papers*, ed. George H. Pollock and John Munder Ross, 493–508. Madison, CT: International Universities Press, 1988.

Milner, Marion. 1952. Aspects of symbolism in comprehension of the not-self. *International Journal of Psycho-Analysis* 33:181–95.
Morales, Sarah Caldwell. 1988. Géza Róheim's theory of the dream origin of myths. *Psychoanalytic Study of Society* 13:7–29
Morgan, William. 1936. Human wolves among the Navaho. *Yale University Publications in Anthropology*, No. 11.New Haven.
Mowat, Farley. 1975. *The People of the Deer.* 2nd ed. Toronto: Seal Books/McClelland & Stewart–Bantam Ltd., 1980.
Muensterberger, Warner. 1964. Remarks on the function of mythology. *Psychoanalytic Study of Society* 3:94–97.
Muensterberger, Warner, and Christopher Nichols. 1974. Róheim and the beginnings of psychoanalytic anthropology. In Róheim. *The Riddle of the Sphinx, or Human Origins*, Trans. R. Money-Kyrle, ix–xxvi. New York: Harper & Row.
Murdoch, John. 1892. Ethnological results of the Point Barrow expedition. *Annual Report of the Bureau of American Ethnology* 9:3–441.
Nagera, Humberto, ed. 1969. *Basic Psychoanalytic Concepts on the Libido Theory.* New York: Basic Books.
Nansen, Fridtjof. 1893. *Eskimo Life.* London: Longmans, Green, & Co.
Natterson, Joseph M. 1966. Theodor Reik. In *Psychoanalytic Pioneers*, ed. Franz Alexander, Samuel Eisenstein, and Martin Grotjahn, 249–264. New York: Basic Books.
Needham, Rodney. 1972. *Belief, Language, and Experience.* Oxford: Basil Blackwell.
Nungak, Zebedee, and Eugene Arima. 1969. *unikkaatuat sanaugargnik atyingualit puvirngniturngmit - eskimo stories from Povungnituk, Quebec, illustrated in soapstone carvings.* National Museums of Canada, Bulletin No. 235, Anthropological Series No. 90. Ottawa: National Museums of Canada.
Oosten, Jarich G. 1976. *The Theoretical Structure of the Religion of the Netsilik and Iglulik.* Meppel: Krips Repro.
Ostow, Mortimer, and Ben-Ami Scharfstein. 1954. *The Need to Believe: The Psychology of Religion.* New York: International Universities Press.
Parsons, Anne. 1969. Is the Oedipus complex universal? The Jones-Malinowski debate revisited and a South Italian 'nuclear complex'. In *Man and His Culture: Psychoanalytic Anthropology after 'Totem and Taboo,'* ed. Warner Muensterberger, 331–84. New York: Taplinger Publishing Company.
Paul, Robert A. 1976. Did the primal crime take place? *Ethos* 4:311–52.
Paulson, Ivar. 1964. The animal guardian: A critical and synthetic review. *History of Religions* 3:202–19.
Pepper, Stephen C. 1935. The root metaphor theory of metaphysics. *Journal of Philosophy* 32:365–74. Reprinted in *Essays on Metaphor*, ed.Warren Shibles, 15–26. Whitewater, WI: The Language Press, 1972.
———. 1942. *World Hypotheses: A Study in Evidence.* Berkeley: University of California Press.
Pfister, Oskar. 1932. Instinctive psychoanalysis among the Navahos. *Journal of Nervous and Mental Disease* 76:234–54.
Pierce, Richard A, ed.1976. A selection from G. I. Davydov: An account of two voyages to America. *Arctic Anthropology* 13(2) :1–30.
Pine, Fred. 1981. In the beginning: Contributions to a psychoanalytic developmental psychology. *International Review of Psycho-Analysis* 8:15–33.
———. 1986. The "symbiotic phase" in light of current infancy research. *Bulletin of the Menninger Clinic* 50(6) :564–69.
———. 1990. *Drive, Ego, Object, and Self: A Synthesis for Clinical Work.* New York: BasicBooks/HarperCollins.

Propp, Vladimir. 1984. *Theory and History of Folklore*. Trans. Ariadna Y. Martin, Richard P. Martin, and several others, ed. Anatoly Liberman. *Theory and History of Literature*. Vol. 5. Minneapolis: University of Minnesota Press.

Radcliffe-Brown, A. R. 1939. Taboo. In *Structure and Function in Primitive Society: Essays and Addresses*. London: Routledge & Kegan Paul, 1952.

Ramanujan, A. K. 1984. The Indian Oedipus. In *Oedipus: A Folklore Casebook*, ed. Lowell Edmunds and Alan Dundes, 234–261. New York and London: Garland Publishing.

Rangell, Leo. 1955. The role of the parent in the Oedipus complex. *Bulletin of the Menninger Clinic* 19:9–15.

Rank, Otto. 1909. The myth of the birth of the hero. In *The Myth of the Birth of the Hero: and Other Writings*, ed. Philip Freund. New York: Vintage Books/Random House, 1964.

———. [1912] 1992. *The Incest Theme in Literature & Legend: Fundamentals of a Psychology of Literary Creation*. Trans. Gregory C. Richter. Baltimore: Johns Hopkins University Press.

———. [1922] 2004. *The Myth of the Birth of the Hero*. 2nd ed. Trans. Gregory Richter and E. James Lieberman. Baltimore: Johns Hopkins University Press.

———. [1924] 1929. *The Trauma of Birth*. New York: Harper & Row, 1973.

———. [1925] 1971. *The Double: A Psychoanalytic Study*. Trans. Harry Tucker, Jr. New York: New American Library.

———. 1932. *Art and Artist: Creative Urge and Personality Development*. Trans. Charles Francis Atkinson. New York: Alfred A. Knopf; reprinted New York and London: W. W. Norton & Company, 1989.

Rank, Otto, and Hanns Sachs. 1913. The significance of psychoanalysis for the humanities. *American Imago* 1964, 21(1–2). Reprinted in *Psychoanalysis as an Art and a Science: A Symposium*, ed. Otto Rank, Hanns Sachs, Bronson Feldman, Benjamin B. Wolman, Harry Slochower, and Ludwig Eidelberg. Detroit: Wayne State University Press, 1968.

Rapaport, David. 1960. *The Structure of Psychoanalytic Theory: A Systematizing Attempt*. New York: International Universities Press.

———. 1967. *The Collected Papers of David Rapaport*, ed. Merton M. Gill. New York: Basic Books.

Rasmussen, Knud. 1908. *The People of the Polar North: A Record*. London: Kegan Paul, Trench, Trubner & Co.

———. 1921. *Greenland by the Polar Sea: The Story of the Thule Expedition from Melville Bay to Cape Morris Jesup*. Trans. Asta and Rowland Kenney. New York: Frederick A. Stokes Company.

———. 1927a. *Across Arctic America: Narrative of the Fifth Thule Expedition*. New York: Greenwood Press, 1969.

———. 1927b. Report of the II Thule-expedition for the exploration of Greenland from Melville Bay to De Long Ford, 1916–1918. *Meddelelser om Grønland*, Vol. 65, No, 1. København: C. A. Reitzel.

———. 1929. *Intellectual Culture of the Iglulik Eskimos*. Report of the Fifth Thule Expedition, Vol. 7, No, 1. København: Gyldendal. Reprinted New York: AMS Press. 1976.

———. 1930. *Observations on the Intellectual Culture of the Caribou Eskimos*. Report of the Fifth Thule Expedition, Vol. 7, No, 2. København: Gyldendal. Reprinted New York: AMS Press. 1976.

———. 1931. *The Netsilik Eskimos: Social Life and Spiritual Culture*. Report of the Fifth Thule Expedition, Vol. 8, Part 1–2. København: Gyldendal. Reprinted New York: AMS Press. 1976.

———. 1932. *Intellectual Culture of the Copper Eskimos*. Report of the Fifth Thule Expedition, Vol. 9. København: Gyldendal. Reprinted New York: AMS Press. 1976.

———. 1938. Knud Rasmussen's posthumous notes on the life and doings of the East Greenlanders in olden times, ed. H. Ostermann. *Meddelelser om Grønland* Vol. 109, No. 1. København: Gyldendal. Reprinted New York: AMS Press. 1976.

———. 1939. Knud Rasmussen's posthumous notes on East Greenland legends and myths, ed. H. Ostermann. *Meddelelser om Grønland* Vol.109, No. 3. København: Reitzel. Reprinted New York: AMS Press, 1976.

———. 1942. *The Mackenzie Eskimos: After Knud Rasmussen's Posthumous Notes*, ed. H. Ostermann. Report of the Fifth Thule Expedition, 10(2).

Reich, Wilhelm. 1949. *Character-Analysis*. 3rd ed. Trans. Theodore P. Wolfe. New York: Noonday Press/Farrar, Straus and Cudahy.

Reichard, Gladys A. 1950. *Navaho Religion: A Study of Symbolism*. 2 vols. New York: Pantheon Books.

Reider, Norman. 1972. Metaphor as interpretation. *International Journal of Psycho-Analysis* 53:463–469.

Reik, Theodor. 1919. Oedipus and the Sphinx. In *Dogma and Compulsion: Psychoanalytic Studies of Religion and Myths*. New York: International Universities Press, 1951; reprinted Westport, CT: Greenwood Press, 1975.

———. 1921. Mythology. *International Journal of Psycho-Analysis* 2:101–05.

———. 1946. *Ritual: Psychoanalytic Studies*. New York: International Universities Press, 1958.

———. 1956. *The Search Within: The Inner Experiences of a Psychoanalyst*. New York: Farrar, Straus & Cudahy.

———. 1957. *Myth and Guilt: The Crime and Punishment of Mankind*. New York: George Braziller, Inc.

———. 1959. *Mystery on the Mountain: The Drama of the Sinai Revelation*. New York: Harper & Brothers.

———. 1960. *The Creation of Woman*. New York: George Braziller, Inc.

———. 1961. *The Temptation*. New York: George Braziller, Inc.

Rink, Henrik. 1875. *Tales and Traditions of the Eskimo*. Montreal: McGill-Queens University Press, 1974.

Rink, Henrik, and Franz Boas. 1889. Eskimo tales and songs. *Journal of American Folk-Lore* 2:123–31.

Rink, Signe. 1898. The girl and the dogs—an Eskimo folk-tale with comments. *American Anthropologist* 11:181–87, 209–15.

Roazen, Paul. 1975. *Freud and His Followers*. New York: Alfred A. Knopf; reprinted New York: Da Capo Press, 1992.

Robinson, Paul A. 1969. *The Freudian Left: Wilhelm Reich, Geza Róheim, Herbert Marcuse*. New York: Harper & Row.

Rodrigué, Emilio. 1956. Notes on symbolism. *International Journal of Psycho-Analysis* 37:147–58.

Rogers, Robert. 1978. *Metaphor: A Psychoanalytic View*. Berkeley: University of California Press.

Róheim, Géza. 1925. *Australian Totemism: A Psycho-Analytic Study in Anthropology*. New York: Humanities Press, 1971.

———. 1932. Psycho-analysis of primitive cultural types. *International Journal of Psycho-Analysis* 13(1–2) :1–224.

———. 1934. *The Riddle of the Sphinx: or Human Origins*. Trans. Roger Money-Kyrle. London: Hogarth Press; reprinted New York: Harper & Row, Publishers, 1974.

———. 1940a. The dragon and the hero. *American Imago* 1(2) :40–69; 1(3) :61–94.

———. 1940b. Society and the individual. *Psychoanalytic Quarterly* 9:526–45.

———. 1941. Myth and folk-tale. *American Imago* 2:266–79.

———. 1943. *The Origin and Function of Culture.* New York: Nervous and Mental Disease Monographs.
———. 1945. *The Eternal Ones of the Dream: A Psychoanalytic Interpretation of Australian Myth and Ritual.* New York: International Universities Press.
———. 1947. Psychoanalysis and anthropology. *Psychoanalysis and the Social Sciences.* Vol. I, ed. Geza Roheim, 9–33. New York: International Universities Press.
———. 1948. The divine child. *Journal of Clinical Psychopathology* 9(2) :309–23.
———. 1950. *Psychoanalysis and Anthropology: Culture, Personality and the Unconscious.* New York: International Universities Press.
———. 1951. Mythology of Arnhem Land. *American Imago* 8:181–87.
———. 1952. *The Gates of the Dream.* New York: International Universities Press.
———. 1954. *Hungarian and Vogul Mythology.* Monographs of the American Ethnological Society, 23. Seattle and London: University of Washington Press.
———. 1972. *The Panic of the Gods: And Other Essays*, ed. Werner Muensterberger. New York: Harper & Row.
———. 1974. *Children of the Desert: Western Tribes of Central Australia.* New York: Basic Books.
Ross, John Munder. 1982. Oedipus revisited: Laius and the "Laius complex." *Psychoanalytic Study of the Child* 37:169–200.
Rubinstein, Benjamin B. 1972. On metaphor and related phenomena. *Psychoanalysis and Contemporary Science*, ed. Robert R. Holt and Emanuel Peterfreund, 1:70–108, New York: Macmillan.
Rudnytsky, Peter L. 1987. *Freud and Oedipus.* New York: Columbia University Press.
———. 1992. Introductory essay. In *The Incest Theme in Literature & Legend: Fundamentals of a Psychology of Literary Creation*, ed. Otto Rank. Trans. Gregory C. Richter. Baltimore: Johns Hopkins University Press, 1992.
Rycroft, Charles. 1977. Is Freudian symbolism a myth? In *Symbols and Sentiments: Cross-Cultural Studies in Symbolism*, ed. Ioan Lewis, 129–40. London and New York: Academic Press.
Sandler, Joseph, with Anna Freud. 1985. *The Analysis of Defense: The Ego and the Mechanisms of Defense Revisited.* New York: International Universities Press.
Sandner, Donald. 1979. *Navaho Symbols of Healing.* New York: Harcourt Brace Jovanovich.
Sapir, Edward, and Harry Hoijer. 1942. *Navaho Texts*, ed. Harry Hoijer. Iowa City: University of Iowa.
Schafer, Roy. 1968. The mechanisms of defence. *International Journal of Psycho-Analysis* 49:49–62.
Segal, Hanna. 1957. Notes on symbol formation. *International Journal of Psycho-Analysis* 38:391–97.
———. 1978. On symbolism. *International Journal of Psycho-Analysis* 59:315–19.
Segal, Robert. 2004. Introduction. In Otto Rank. *The Myth of the birth of the Hero.* 2nd ed. 1922 in German. Trans. Gregory Richter and E. James Lieberman. Baltimore: Johns Hopkins University Press.
Seznec, Jean. 1953. *The Survival of the Pagan Gods: The Mythological Tradition and Its Place in Renaissance Humanism and Art.* Princeton: Princeton University Press/Bollingen Foundation, 1972.
Sharpe, Ella Freeman. 1937. *Dream Analysis: A Practical Handbook for Psycho-Analysts.* London: Hogarth Press; reprinted New York: Brunner/Mazel, 1978.
Siegelman, Ellen Y. 1990. *Metaphor and Meaning in Psychotherapy.* New York and London: Guilford Press.
Silberer, Herbert. 1909. Report on a method of eliciting and observing certain symbolic hallucination-phenomena. In *Organization and Pathology of Thought: Selected Sources*, ed. David Rapaport, 195–207. New York: Columbia University Press, 1951.

———. 1912. On symbol-formation. In *Organization and Pathology of Thought*, 208–333.
———. 1914. *Hidden Symbolism of Alchemy and the Occult Arts*. (First English title: Problems of Mysticism and Its Symbolism.) Trans. Smith Ely Jelliffe, London: Moffat, Yard, 1917. Reprinted New York: Dover Publications, Inc., 1971.
———. 1920–21. The Origin and the Meaning of the Symbols of Freemasonry, Parts I-III. *Psyche and Eros* 1(1920) :17–24, 84–97; 2(1921) :81–89, 299–309.
Skeels, Dell R. 1964. Eros and Thanatos in Nez Perce River mythology. *American Imago* 21:102–110.
Slater, Philip E. 1968. *The Glory of Hera: Greek Mythology and the Greek Family.* Boston: Beacon Press.
Slochower, Harry. 1970. Psychoanalytic distinction between myth and mythopoesis. *Journal of the American Psychoanalytic Association* 18:150–63.
Spiro, Melford E. 1951. Some Ifaluk myths and folk tales. *Journal of American Folklore* 64:289–302.
———. 1973. The Oedipus complex in Burma. *Journal of Nervous and Mental Disease* 157:389–95.
———. 1982. *Oedipus in the Trobriands*. Chicago: University of Chicago Press.
———. 1984. Psychoanalysis and cultural relativism: The Trobriand case. In *Psychoanalysis: The Vital Issues, Volume I: Psychoanalysis as an Intellectual Discipline*, ed. John E. Gedo and George H. Pollock, 165–81. New York: International Universities Press.
Stanner, W. E. H. 1956. The dreaming, an Australian world view. Reprinted in *Cultural and Social Anthropology: Selected Readings*, ed. Peter B. Hammond, 288–98. New York: Macmillan Company, 1964.
Steiner, John. 1985. Turning a blind eye: The cover up for Oedipus. *International Review of Psycho-Analysis* 12:161–72.
———. 1990. The retreat from truth to omnipotence in Sophocles' *Oedipus at Colonus*. *International Review of Psycho-Analysis* 17:227–37.
Stephens, William N. 1952. *The Oedipus Complex: Cross-Cultural Evidence.* New York: Free Press of Glencoe.
Stern, Max M. 1964. Ego psychology, myth and rite: Remarks about the relationship of the individual and the group. *Psychoanalytic Study of Society* 3:71–93.
Suttie, Ian D. 1935. *The Origins of Love and Hate.* London: Kegan Paul, Trench, Trubner, Reprinted London: Free Association Boosk, 1988.
Symington, Neville. 1993. *Narcissism: A New Theory.* London: Karnac Books.
Szajnberg, Nathan. 1985–1986. Übertragung, metaphor, and transference in psychoanalytic psychotherapy. *International Journal of Psychoanalytic Psychotherapy* 11:53–69.
Tarachow, Sidney. 1964. Mythology and ego psychology: Introductory remarks. *Psychoanalytic Study of Society* 3:9–12.
Thalbitzer, William. 1921. The Ammassalik Eskimo: Contributions to the ethnology of the East Greenland natives. III. Language and folklore. *Meddelelser om Grønland*, Vol. 40, No. 3. København: C A. Reitzel. Reprinted New York: AMS Press, 1979.
Thass-Thienemann, Theodore. 1957. Oedipus and the Sphinx: The linguistic approach to unconscious fantasies. *Psychoanalytic Review* 44:10–33.
Thompson, Stith. 1929. *Tales of the North American Indians: Selected and Annotated.* Bloomington: Indiana University Press, 1966.
Tourney, Garfield. 1965. Freud and the Greeks: A study of the influence of classical Greek mythology and philosophy upon the development of Freudian thought. *Journal of the History of the Behavioral Sciences* 1:67–85.
Turner, Lucien M. 1894. Ethnology of the Ungava District, Hudson Bay Territory. *Anthropological Report of the Bureau of American Ethnology* 11(2) :159–350.
Turner, Mark. 1987. *Death is the Mother of Beauty: Mind, Metaphor, Criticism.* Chicago: University of Chicago Press.

Tylor, Sir E. B. 1960. *Anthropology*, abr. Ann Arbor: University of Michigan Press.
Vaidyanathan, T. G., and Jeffrey J. Kripal 1999. *Vishnu on Freud's Desk: A Reader in Psychoanalysis and Hinduism*. Delhi: Oxford University Press.
Vellacott, Philip. 1971. *Sophocles and Oedipus: A Study of* Oedipus Tyrannus *with a New Translation*. Ann Arbor: University of Michigan Press.
Vernon, Thomas S. 1971–1972. The Laios complex: 'generational hatred.' *Intercom. University of Arkansas* 8(2): 2, 5.
———. 1972. The Laius complex. *Humanist* 32(6) :27–28
Victor, George. 1978. Interpretations couched in mythical imagery. *International Journal of Psychoanalytic Psychotherapy* 7:225–239.
von Sydow, Carl Wilhelm. 1948. *Selected Papers on Folklore*. Copenhagen: Rosenkilde & Bagger.
von Wrangell, Ferdinand Petrovich. 1970. The inhabitants of the northwest coast of America. Trans. and ed. James W. VanStone. *Arctic Anthropology* 6(2) :5–20.
Voth, Harold M. 1970. The analysis of metaphor. *Journal of the American Psychoanalytic Association* 18:599–621.
Wälder, Robert. 1937. The problem of the genesis of psychical conflict in earliest infancy: Remarks on a paper by Joan Riviere. *International Journal of Psycho–Analysis* 18:406–473.
Wallace, Edwin R, IV 1983. *Freud and Anthropology: A History and Reappraisal*. New York: International Universities Press.
Wax, Murray L. 1990. Malinowski, Freud and Oedipus. *International Journal of Psycho-Analysis* 17:47–60.
Weigert-Vowinkel, Edith. 1938. The cult and mythology of the magna mater from the standpoint of psychoanalysis. *Psychiatry* 1:347–78.
Williamson, Robert G. 1974. *Eskimo Underground: Socio-Cultural Change in the Central Canadian Arctic*. Uppsala: Almqvist & Wiksell.
Winter, David G. 1975. Introduction. In *The Don Juan Legend*, ed. Otto Rank. Princeton, NJ: Princeton University Press.
Worster, W. W. 1925. Eskimo folk-lore and myth. *Edinburgh Review* 242:94–107.
Wright, Kenneth J. T. 1976. Metaphor and symptom: A study of integration and its failure. *International Review of Psycho-Analysis* 3:97–109.
Wyman, Leland C., with Haile Berard. 1975. *The Mountainway of the Navajo*. Tucson: University of Arizona Press.
Wyman, Leland C., Hill, W. W., and Iva Osanai. 1942. Navajo eschatology. *University of New Mexico Bulletin*, Vol. 4, No. 1.
Wyman, Leland C., and Clyde Kluckhohn. 1938. Navaho classification of their song ceremonials. *Memoirs of the American Anthropological Association*, No. 50.
Zimmer, Heinrich. 1946. *Myths and Symbols in Indian Art and Civilization*. Princeton: Princeton/Bollingen Paperback, 1972.
Zulliger, Hans. 1966. Oskar Pfister 1873–1956: Psychoanalysis and faith. In *Psychoanalytic Pioneers*, ed. Franz Alexander, Samuel Eisenstein, and Martin Grotjahn, 169–179. New York: Basic Books.

INDEX

E

F

G

H

I

P

R

S

T

U

V

W

Z